KU-015-184

CHOCOLATE HEAVEN

Chocolate Heaven

The Ultimate Indulgence

Elizabeth Wolf Cohen
and
Valerie Barrett

APPLE

540396

MORAY DISTRICT COUNCIL
DEPARTMENT OF
LEISURE AND LIBRARIES
641.6374

A QUINTET BOOK

Published by the Apple Press
6 Blundell Street
London N7 9BH

Copyright © 1995 Quintet Publishing Limited.
All rights reserved. No part of this publication may be reproduced, stored
in a retrieval system or transmitted in any form or by any means,
electronic, mechanical, photocopying, recording or otherwise, without the
permission of the copyright holder.

ISBN 1-85076-631-2

The material in this book previously appeared in *The Chocolate Cookbook*
by Elizabeth Wolf Cohen, and *The Chocolate Book* by Valerie Barrett.

This book was designed and produced by
Quintet Publishing Limited
6 Blundell Street
London N7 9BH

Creative Director: Richard Dewing
Designer: Isobel Gillan
Editor: Diana Vowles

Typeset in Great Britain by
Central Southern Typesetters, Eastbourne
Manufactured by Eray Scan Pte Ltd, Singapore
Printed by Star Standard Industries (Pte) Ltd, Singapore

Contents

ℐNTRODUCTION

THE HISTORY OF CHOCOLATE

Smooth, rich chocolate in its many present day variations has its origins in a simple brown bean. The cocoa bean grows on the cocoa tree and it is believed that the trees originally grew wild in the Amazon. It is probable that when the Mayans migrated to the Yucatan in about AD 600 they established the first cocoa plantations. The Aztecs also used the beans and would have carried them on their travels in Central America.

The beans fulfilled two purposes. They were used as currency: it is said that 10 beans would buy a rabbit and 100 would buy a slave! The other use to which the cocoa bean was put was as the basis of a bitter, foamy drink which had religious and ceremonial significance. This drink, called *chocolatl* (bitter water) was made by mixing roasted ground beans with water or wine which was then beaten until frothy.

Christopher Columbus has been credited with discovering America and as being the first European to see cocoa beans and probably to taste the drink. He returned to the Spanish court with some beans, but they aroused little interest, perhaps because Columbus himself was more interested in his search for new routes to the East. Nothing more happened on the chocolate front for about 17 years until the Spanish explorer Cortez conquered Mexico in 1519. Cortez and his Spanish Conquistadors were invited to the magnificent Aztec court of the Emperor Montezuma. Although Cortez disliked the drink, he was impressed by the way it was served in ornate golden goblets and with the quantity drunk by the Emperor and his intimates. He was also quick to recognize the value of the bean as a currency. Cortez therefore established his own cocoa plantation under the Spanish flag. When the Spanish left Mexico,

LEFT *Classic Devil's Food Cake*

they took some beans with them and planted them in various places as they travelled. Once home, Cortez introduced the chocolate drink to the Spanish court. As the drink was pungent and bitter the Spaniards added sugar and vanilla to it. These additions made the drink much more palatable and it quickly became very popular at court and in high society. The Spanish began to plant more and more cocoa overseas, but they kept the secret of its preparation for almost 100 years.

In 1606 an Italian called Antonio Carlotti took the recipe to Italy. From then on the drink spread throughout Europe. When Anne of Austria married Louis XIII of France she brought her own chocolate with her and when the Spanish princess Marie Thérèse married Louis XIV, chocolate was drunk at court, a royal chocolate maker was appointed and chocolate drinking became the rage. Coffee houses, which were already established meeting-places in England, were now joined by chocolate houses. These places were the precursors of our present-day cafés and bars and they were frequented by politicians, writers and socialites.

The first chocolate factory in America was set up in New England in 1765. Similar factories were also springing up in Europe; Dr Joseph Fry was the first Englishman to manufacture chocolate in a big way. The real breakthrough came in 1828 when a Dutchman called C Van Houten patented a process whereby cocoa powder and extract cocoa butter could be obtained from the cocoa mass. Up until this time the whole bean had been ground and used, resulting in a "fatty" drink. Van Houten's cocoa press squeezed out some of the cocoa butter, leaving behind what we now know as cocoa powder. Twenty years later Joseph Fry discovered how to combine the extracted cocoa butter with the chocolate liquor and sugar to make "eating" chocolate, and in Switzerland, in 1875, Daniel Peter added condensed milk to chocolate and marketed the first solid milk chocolate bar.

A few years later Rodolphe Lindt invented a way of refining chocolate. As long as chocolate was made into a drink it didn't matter if it had lumps and gritty bits as these tended to dissolve or sink with the addition of liquid. However, a solid chocolate bar was a different matter. Lindt's process, which became known as "conching", consisted of putting the chocolate in heated drums for about 72 hours and rubbing it between rollers or discs. This process gives a silky smoothness to chocolate, allowing it to be poured into different moulds rather than just pressed into "cakes".

Since then, the technological changes in the manufacture of chocolate and chocolate products have come fast and furious. From being a luxury that only the rich could afford, chocolate is now an everyday commodity that we take for granted.

How Chocolate is Grown and Made

The cocoa bean which gives us both cocoa and chocolate is grown in pods on the cocoa tree *(Theobroma cacao)*. The first cocoa trees probably originated in the Amazon forest more than 4000 years ago. Because the tree requires a tropical climate, it is cultivated only in West Africa, northern and central South America, the Caribbean and some parts of Asia between the tropics of Cancer and Capricorn.

The cocoa tree is extremely sensitive and so the young seeds are grown in special nurseries. After a few months they are transplanted to the cocoa plantation. They need protection from wind and excessive sunlight. This is often provided by banana, coconut or lemon trees, known as "cocoa mothers", which are planted nearby.

By the time the tree is four or five years old it has dark glossy leaves and ripe fruit in the form of pods growing on both the branches and the trunk. An evergreen, the tree is not dissimilar in size and shape to an English apple tree. The pods are about 7.5–10 cm (3–4 inches) wide and 15–25 cm (6–10 inches) long and are elongated ovals in shape. When young they are a green or red colour and as they ripen the outer shells become hard and turn golden or bright red. Inside the pod are between 20 and 50 plump almond-shaped seeds surrounded by a whitish pulp. These seeds are the precious cocoa beans.

On most plantations there are two harvest seasons, each lasting about three months. The pods are cut down from the trees with large steel knives or machetes, collected in baskets and taken to be opened. Once they are split apart the beans and pulp are scooped out. At first the beans are creamy beige in colour, but as they are exposed to the air they change to purple. The pulp and the seeds are put into large heaps either on the ground or in boxes or baskets, covered with leaves and left to ferment. The white pulp ferments and produces alcohol and other by-products. The temperature rises and kills off the germ in the cocoa beans so that they cannot sprout, and starts a chain of chemical reactions that remove the bitterness and develop the characteristic chocolate flavour. At the end of fermentation, which can take from two to six days, the beans have turned brown and have become separated from the pulp. They are still wet and have to be spread out in the sun or dried with hot-air blowers to prevent them from rotting. At this stage, checks are made for defects, such as mould or insect damage. The sun gives the beans an even deeper colour and a more aromatic flavour.

The beans are then put into sacks and sent all over the world to various processing plants.

On arrival at the factory, the beans are cleaned and sorted. They are then roasted in a similar way to coffee beans. During roasting the beans become darker brown,

the shell becomes brittle and the beans take on their full "chocolate" aroma. The roasted beans are now put into a machine which cracks them open and an artificial wind or winnower blows away the brittle shell, leaving behind the cocoa "nibs".

The nibs are ground between rollers to produce a thick dark paste or "chocolate liquor" called the "mass". It hardens on cooling and is sometimes formed into bars at this stage to be sold as unsweetened baking chocolate. This mass or chocolate liquor is the basis of all chocolate and cocoa products.

To make cocoa powder, the chocolate liquor is poured into a press. A good percentage of the cocoa butter (a fatty substance which is found in the bean) is pressed out. This leaves a solid, dry cake which is then crushed, ground and sieved. The end result of this process is cocoa powder. Cocoa powder is sold just as it is, or it can be mixed with a variety of ingredients such as sugar, starches and milk to produce drinking chocolate or chocolate malted drinks.

Whereas cocoa is made by extracting cocoa butter from the chocolate liquor, chocolate is made by adding extra cocoa butter to it. Adding sugar produces "plain" chocolate; adding milk and sugar produces "milk" chocolate. "White" chocolate is made from cocoa butter only, with the addition of sugar and milk.

When the various ingredients are added to the liquor they are blended in a mixing machine. At this point the mixture is still gritty, so it goes through a series of heavy rollers called a refiner. After this the chocolate is smooth, but to make it really silky on the tongue, it goes through a final stirring treatment known as "conching". This takes place in large drums or conches (from the Spanish *concha*, meaning shell) in which the chocolate is heated and kneaded with rollers. After conching, the liquid chocolate is tempered or cooled so that the fat begins to harden and the chocolate can then be moulded. The filled moulds are cooled, the chocolate removed, wrapped and sent to the stores. So ends the journey from cocoa bean to chocolate bar.

TYPES OF CHOCOLATE

Unsweetened Chocolate

Also known as "cooking", "baking" or "baker's chocolate", this is most widely used in the US and Canada and although it is exported it is not always available in Great Britain. The nearest substitute is always to use 3 tablespoons cocoa and 1 tablespoon fat to replace 25 g (1 oz) unsweetened chocolate. The flavour of unsweetened chocolate is bitter, intense and full-bodied, as it has no sugar or flavourings added.

Bitter Chocolate

Bitter chocolate is available in some delicatessens (Van Houten, Lindt and Suchard are popular brands) and it can be used instead of plain chocolate for a strong flavour.

Couverture Chocolate

Couverture chocolate contains a high proportion of cocoa butter, which makes it very smooth and glossy. As it has a very brittle texture it needs "tempering" before use (see page 13). This type of chocolate is used normally by professionals. However, it is excellent for coating and moulding and well worth buying if you do a lot of chocolate cooking.

Milk Chocolate

Milk chocolate has a much milder flavour than plain as some of the chocolate has been replaced by milk solids. It is best to use this chocolate only in recipes that specifically call for it.

Chocolate Cake Covering or "Coating" Chocolate

This should not be confused with plain or milk chocolate as it has a certain amount of the cocoa butter replaced by coconut, palm kernel oil or some other vegetable fat. It is much cheaper than plain chocolate and, because it is very easily melted, it is easier to handle. It is good for decorative chocolate recipes and for covering or coating cakes, as it does not streak. The only disadvantage is that the flavour is not as strong as that of plain chocolate.

Dipping Chocolate

This chocolate makes a good alternative to couverture chocolate. It contains a high proportion of vegetable fat and is good for dipping and moulding.

Plain Chocolate

Plain eating chocolate has a good strong flavour and is the most suited for use in cake, dessert and sweet recipes. Plain chocolate is made with chocolate liquor, cocoa butter, vegetable fats, sugar and flavourings.

Cocoa Powder

This is chocolate from which the cocoa butter has been removed, before being ground into a powder. Dutch cocoa powder, if available, is darker and slightly less bitter than most as it has been treated with an alkali. Cocoa can be used dry and sieved with other dry ingredients such as flour or icing sugar before being incorporated into a recipe. In some recipes it is better to mix the cocoa to a paste with hot water, thus breaking down the starch cells before cooking.

Drinking Chocolate

Drinking chocolate is cocoa with a high proportion of sugar. It has a mild, very sweet flavour. Apart from its obvious use in drinks it can be useful as a coating on such things as truffles.

White Chocolate

This is not really a chocolate at all. It is made from milk, sugar and cocoa butter or another vegetable fat. It is not normally used for cooking, but if you do wish to experiment take great care when melting it as it can very easily become tight and grainy.

COOKING WITH CHOCOLATE

Cooking with chocolate as the main ingredient can be quite spectacular, especially when other good-quality ingredients are used. To prevent disappointment, you must remember to treat chocolate with TLC: tender loving care.

Melting Chocolate

There are several different ways to melt chocolate, but if you wish to avoid ending up with a solid mass there are a few rules which must be observed. Any equipment used must be perfectly dry because any stray drops of water will cause the chocolate to thicken and stiffen. For the same reason, never cover chocolate when it is being, or has already been, melted. If you do end up with a solid mass, try stirring in a little vegetable oil and mix very well. Butter or margarine will not do as they contain some water. The second thing to remember is *never* to rush the melting process. A watched pot never boils and the temptation is to turn up the heat and speed up the process. Unfortunately this will ruin the flavour and texture of the chocolate. It is best to grate or chop the chocolate before melting for a smooth result.

Direct Heat Method

This method is only used when the chocolate is combined with butter, sugar or milk, or similar ingredients, as when making some sweets and sauces. The mixture should always be stirred over a very gentle heat. As soon as the mixture has melted it should be removed from the heat to prevent the chocolate over-cooking and becoming "grainy".

Double Boiler Method

This is probably one of the best and easiest methods of melting chocolate. If you do not possess a double boiler, one can easily be made by placing a heatproof bowl over a saucepan. The bowl should fit securely on the pan so that neither steam nor water can escape. The water in the saucepan should never touch the bottom of the bowl. Place the chocolate in the bowl. Allow the water in the saucepan to come to the boil and place the bowl on top. Turn off the heat under the saucepan and leave to stand for a while until the chocolate is melted.

Oven Method

Chocolate may be melted in an ovenproof bowl in a very low oven (110°C/225°F/Gas ¼). If the oven has been in use for another purpose and has been turned off, it makes sense to use the lingering heat to melt the chocolate. When the chocolate has almost melted it should be removed and stirred until smooth.

Microwave Oven Method

Microwave ovens are very handy for melting chocolate, especially small quantities, quickly and safely. The chocolate should be broken into small pieces and put into a glass bowl. Microwave, uncovered, until almost melted. The manufacturer's instructions should be followed as the timing and power setting will vary according to the machine.

On average, 75 g (3 oz) chocolate will melt in 1–1½ minutes. It is important to stir the chocolate just before the end of the cooking time to see if the chocolate has melted and thus prevent overcooking.

Double boiler method

How to "Temper" Couverture Chocolate

Generally speaking couverture chocolate is only used by professionals and so is not readily available in shops. However, if you wish to do a lot of chocolate cookery, especially dipping or using moulds, it is worth getting hold of some. Because couverture has a high cocoa butter content it flows and coats excellently. Couverture chocolate must be tempered before using. To do this you will need a thermometer. Break up the chocolate and melt by the double boiler method. Heat the chocolate to a temperature of 38–46°C (100–115°F). Stir well during this heating process. The chocolate then has to be cooled. To do this, remove the bowl to a pan of cold water and cool to 27–28°C (80–82°F), stirring thoroughly. Return the chocolate to the double boiler and reheat to 31–32°C (88–90°F). Stir all the time and do not exceed this final temperature. The chocolate is now ready to be used. If there is chocolate left over at the end, it can be reheated without further tempering.

Chocolate for Dipping

Delicious sweetmeats such as marzipan, caramel, fudge and crystallized or fresh fruits can all be dipped in chocolate. Use either tempered couverture or dipping or plain chocolate. Heat in a double boiler. The ideal temperature for dipping is 36–43°C (92–110°F). The temperature should never exceed 49°C (120°F). The chocolate should be in a bowl deep enough for the confection to be totally covered. Using a special dipping fork, fondue fork or thin skewer, lower the confection into the chocolate. Turn it over and then lift out the chocolate, tapping the fork on the edge of the bowl to shake off the excess chocolate. Place the chocolate on a tray lined with greaseproof paper. The dipping fork can be used to decorate the top of the chocolates before they set. Lay the fork on the surface of the chocolate and lift it gently to create raised ridges.

Using Moulds

Special moulds can be bought to make eggs, animals (such as rabbits or mice), boxes and so on. They are available in metal or plastic. The plastic ones are cheaper and easier to use in that you can see when the chocolate has shrunk from the sides. The mould must be extremely clean so the chocolate does not stick and has a shiny surface. Wash and rinse the mould and dry very well. Polish well with a soft cloth, kitchen towel or cotton wool.

It is best to use a chocolate that will set hard, so always choose dipping, couverture or plain, good-quality eating chocolate. Melt the chocolate over hot water. The amount will vary according to the size of the

mould. Very small moulds will only need one layer, but larger ones will need two, three or four layers. The larger the mould, the thicker the chocolate layer needs to be. Pour the melted chocolate into the mould. Tilt and rotate the mould so that the chocolate coats it evenly. Tip out any excess chocolate. Turn the mould upside down on to a tray lined with greaseproof paper. Put it in a cool place (*not* the refrigerator) until the first layer is just firm to the touch. Repeat as above for subsequent layers. Leave the chocolate to set hard. The chocolate should have shrunk away from the mould when it is ready.

Very carefully scrape away any chocolate that has gone over the edge of the mould. Gently pull or shake the shape out of the mould. Be careful not to mark the outside with fingerprints! Place the shapes on grease-proof paper. To stick two halves together, as for an Easter egg, brush a little melted chocolate round the rim and press the two halves together. Melted chocolate or royal icing can be used to pipe over any joins on the outside.

STORING CHOCOLATE

Chocolate should be kept in a cool dry place. Contrary to popular belief the refrigerator is not the best place to store chocolate other than for short periods during hot weather. When refrigerated, chocolate will absorb odours very easily and also may collect a film of moisture on the surface, so wrap the chocolate in foil then in a plastic bag if you wish to refrigerate it. Let the chocolate stand at room temperature before unwrapping and using as this should prevent moisture condensing on the surface.

If chocolate is stored in very warm conditions the cocoa butter or sugar crystals in it may rise to the surface, giving a greyish white "bloom". This is completely harmless and although it detracts from the appearance it does not affect the flavour of the chocolate. The bloom will disappear on melting so the chocolate is quite suitable for cooking.

If you wish to keep chocolate for a longer time in hot conditions, then it is best to freeze it. Again, make sure it is tightly wrapped. Remove it from the freezer the night before you need it, and allow it to thaw completely before unwrapping it. The freezer is an especially good place to store chocolate decorations such as squares, leaves, and so on. These can then be used any time to garnish cakes and desserts and only need a few hours to thaw.

If kept in the correct conditions, plain chocolate should keep for one year and milk chocolate for about six months.

USEFUL EQUIPMENT FOR CHOCOLATE COOKING

Grater

For grating chocolate, you will need a stainless steel box or conical-shaped grater with varied cutting edges.

Potato Peeler

A potato peeler is used for making chocolate curls. The type that has a fixed blade is best.

Skewers or Cocktail Sticks

These are useful for dipping or the lifting and placing of delicate chocolate decorations.

Dipping Forks

These are usually about 20 cm (8 inches) long, made of stainless steel with wooden handles. They are available in a variety of shapes, from two, three and four prongs to round, spiral or triangular shapes. As well as dipping, the forks can be used for marking designs on top of the chocolates.

Double Boiler

Best made of stainless steel or enamelled steel, this consists of two pans, one made to rest on top and slightly inside the other. Hot water is placed in the bottom pan and the chocolate is melted in the top.

Sugar Boiling Thermometer

Made of brass, the thermometer should be well graduated up to 210°C (400°F). It is essential for certain sweetmeat recipes and also for tempering couverture chocolate.

Cutters

You will need a selection of various sizes and shapes in steel or plastic. There are very many available now and some make lovely chocolate decorations.

Sweet and Cake Cases

These are available in different sizes and qualities. If they are to be used for making chocolate cups, choose foil if you can, or else a sturdy paper type.

Piping Bags and Nozzles

For piping chocolate, medium or small bags are best. In fact, for piping small amounts of chocolate in decorative work it is better to make bags from greaseproof or waxed paper. Star, rope and plain nozzles are the most useful to have.

Marble Slab

Not essential, but useful to have for chocolate work as it keeps everything cool.

Chocolate Draining Tray

This is similar to a cooling rack, but with a smaller wire mesh.

Greaseproof Paper

Greaseproof paper is ideal for lining pans or baking trays when working with chocolate.

Moulds

Several different types are available. One type is made of tin, with two halves which clip together when setting. This type makes a solid mould. Other types come in one "half" of a shape and are used to make hollow moulds.

Icing Comb

Made of plastic or metal, this is useful for making ridged designs on chocolate, such as when making florentines.

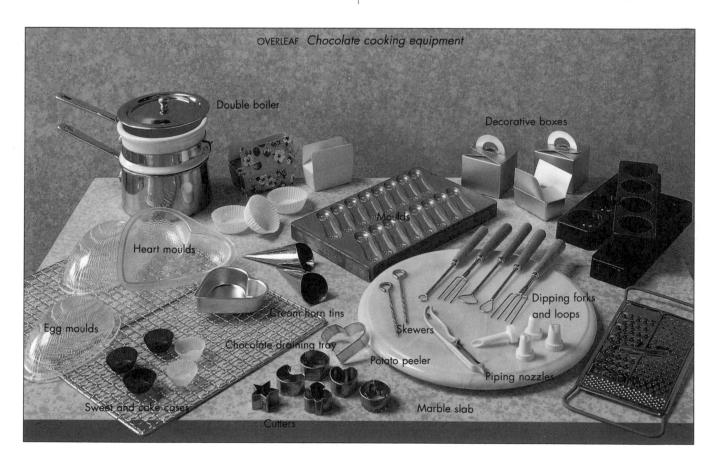

OVERLEAF *Chocolate cooking equipment*

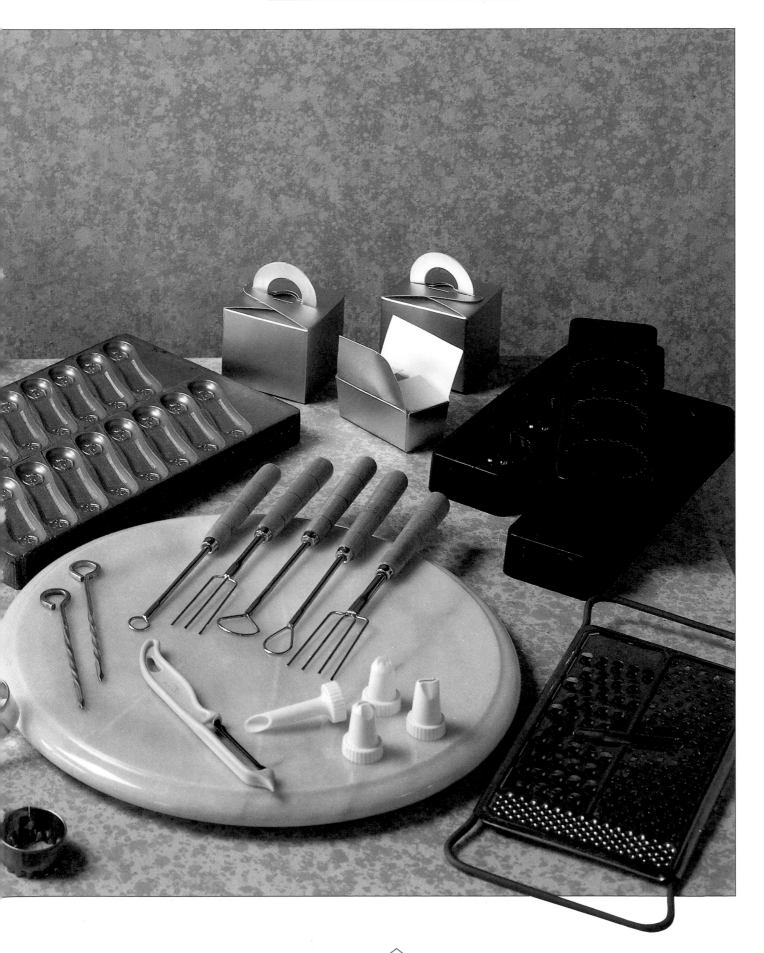

MAKING CHOCOLATE DECORATIONS

Grated Chocolate

Chill the chocolate and then rub it across a hand grater. Use either the fine grater or the large grater, depending on the dish you wish to garnish. To prevent clogging, brush the grater every now and then with a dry pastry brush.

Chocolate Scrolls

Melt some cooking or plain chocolate and spread out on a cool work surface to a thickness of about 3 mm (⅛ inch). Cool until set, but not hard. Hold a long firm knife at an angle of 45° under the chocolate and push it away from you, scraping off long curls.

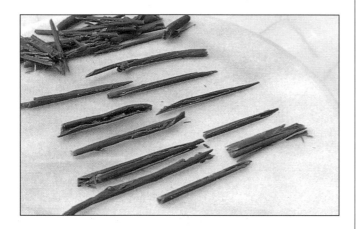

Chocolate Curls

Use chocolate at room temperature (if the chocolate is too cold the curls will break, and if it is too hot they will not curl at all). It is best to use a very thick bar of chocolate. Holding the bar over a plate, draw the blade of a vegetable peeler along the edge and allow the curls to fall on to the plate. Use a toothpick to lift the curls on to the dish to be decorated.

Chocolate Caraque

Melt and spread some chocolate as for chocolate scrolls. Place a sharp-pointed, long-bladed knife on the surface of the chocolate. Keep the tip of the knife securely in one place. Holding the knife at a slight angle, scrape in a quarter circle movement to produce long, thin, slightly cone-shaped curls.

Chopped Chocolate

Use chocolate at room temperature. Break into small pieces and place on a chopping board. Using a sharp chopping knife, chop into the size required. Chocolate may also be chopped quite successfully in a food processor.

Chocolate Squares, Triangles, Rectangles and Wedges

Melt cooking or plain chocolate and spread evenly on greaseproof paper. Leave to set. Using a ruler, mark into squares or rectangles. Cut with a sharp knife. The squares may be cut diagonally to form triangles and the rectangles cut diagonally to form wedges.

Chocolate Cups

Use two thicknesses of paper cake or sweet cases. (If you can obtain foil cases a single layer only is necessary.) Melt the chocolate and brush on the bottom and up the sides of the cases. Repeat this process until a thick layer is obtained. Carefully turn upside down onto greaseproof paper. Chill until hard. Peel the paper cases away from the chocolate and fill as desired.

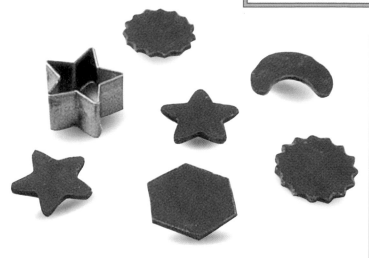

Chocolate Cut-outs

Melt cooking or plain chocolate and spread evenly on greaseproof paper. Leave to set. Using cocktail biscuit or cookie cutters, stamp out shapes, such as hearts, crescents, stars, animals, letters and so on.

Piped Designs

Trace the chosen design lightly on a piece of greaseproof paper. Melt the chocolate and pour into a piping bag, fitted with a small plain nozzle. Follow the outline of the design first. Either fill in the centres with solid chocolate or pipe a "lace" infill. Ideas for piped designs:

Holly leaves: Pipe outlines and then fill in centres.

Simple flower shapes: Pipe any flower shape that appeals to you, such as a daisy.

Chocolate filigree fans: Outline a fan shape and fill in with "lace" work.

Butterflies: Cut greaseproof paper into small squares. Pipe chocolate on to the paper in a butterfly outline. Fill in the wings with additional lines. Leave until beginning to set. Transfer to an upturned egg carton, placing the butterfly between the cups so it is bent in the centre in the shape of a butterfly. Chill. Carefully remove the paper and position on the chosen dish.

Chocolate Leaves

Select non-toxic fresh leaves with clearly defined veins, such as rose, bay, ivy, strawberry or mint. Wash the leaves and pat dry. Melt some chocolate on a heatproof plate over a pan of hot water. Holding the leaf by the stem, carefully dip the veined side only into the chocolate. Alternatively, brush the chocolate on the leaf with a small paintbrush. Wipe off any chocolate that may have run onto the front of the leaf. Place on greaseproof paper to set. When the chocolate is completely hard, carefully pull off the leaf by the stem.

Chocolate Horns

To make chocolate horns you will need cream horn tins. Make sure the tins are clean and dry, and polish the inside well with paper towels. Pour a little melted chocolate into the tin, and tilt and turn it until evenly coated. Repeat this process until a thick layer of chocolate is coating the inside of the mould. Leave to set. The chocolate should shrink slightly away from the mould when hard and can be carefully eased out with the point of a knife.

Chocolate-coated ice cream cones can be made in a similar manner. After coating the insides of the ice cream cones with chocolate they can be placed in the freezer for about 10 minutes to harden. They should then be filled with scoops of ice cream and eaten immediately.

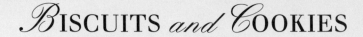BISCUITS *and* COOKIES

Chocolate Crackle Tops

MAKES ABOUT 38

200 g (7 oz) plain chocolate, chopped
90 g (3½ oz) unsalted butter
150 g (5 oz) caster sugar
3 eggs
15 ml (1 tbsp) vanilla essence
175 g (6 oz) plain flour
25 g (1 oz) cocoa powder
½ tsp baking powder
¼ tsp salt
175-225 g (6-8 oz) icing sugar for coating

SWEET SUCCESS

These biscuits are best eaten as fresh as possible, but they will last for several days in an airtight container.

◆ In a saucepan over low heat, melt the chocolate and butter, stirring frequently until smooth. Remove from the heat. Stir in the sugar and continue stirring for 2-3 minutes, until the sugar dissolves. Add the eggs, 1 at a time, beating well after each addition, then stir in the vanilla essence.

◆ Into a bowl, sift together the flour, cocoa powder, baking powder and salt. Gradually stir into the chocolate mixture in batches just until blended. Cover the dough and refrigerate for 2-3 hours or overnight, until the dough is cold and holds its shape.

◆ Preheat the oven to 170°C (325°F, Gas Mark 3). Grease 2 or more large baking sheets. Place 150 g (5 oz) icing sugar in a small, deep bowl. Using a small ice cream scoop, about 2.5 cm (1 inch) in diameter, or a teaspoon, scoop the cold dough into small balls.

◆ Between the palms of your hands, roll the dough into 4 cm (1½ inch) balls. Drop the balls, 1 at a time, into icing sugar and roll until heavily coated. Remove each ball with a slotted spoon and tap against the side of the bowl to remove excess sugar. Place on baking sheets 4 cm (1½ inches) apart. Use more icing sugar as necessary; you may need to cook in batches.

◆ Bake the biscuits for 10-12 minutes, or until top of biscuit feels slightly firm when touched with fingertip; do not overbake or biscuits will be dry. Transfer the baking sheets to a wire rack for 2-3 minutes, just until the biscuits are set. With a palette knife, transfer the biscuits to a wire rack to cool completely.

Chocolate Chunk Chocolate Drops

MAKES ABOUT 18

175 g (6 oz) plain chocolate, chopped
100 g (4 oz) unsalted butter, cut
into pieces
2 eggs
100 g (4 oz) sugar
40 g (1½ oz) brown sugar
40 g (1½ oz) flour
25 g (1 oz) cocoa powder
1 tsp baking powder
10 ml (2 tsp) vanilla essence
¼ tsp salt
90 g (3½ oz) pecans, toasted
and chopped
175 g (6 oz) plain chocolate chips
100g (4 oz) good-quality white
chocolate, chopped into 5 mm
(¼ inch) pieces
100g (4 oz) good-quality milk
chocolate, chopped into 5 mm
(¼ inch) pieces

◆ Preheat the oven to 170°C (325°F, Gas Mark 3). Grease 2 large baking sheets. In a medium saucepan over low heat, melt the chocolate and butter, stirring frequently until smooth. Remove from the heat to cool slightly.

◆ With an electric mixer, beat the eggs and sugars until thick and pale, 2-3 minutes. Gradually pour in the melted chocolate, beating until well blended. Beat in the flour, cocoa powder, baking powder, vanilla essence and salt just until blended. Stir in the nuts, chocolate chips and chocolate pieces.

◆ Drop heaping tablespoonfuls of dough on the baking sheets at least 10 cm (4 inches) apart, flattening the dough slightly, trying to keep about a 7.5 cm (3 inch) circle; you will only get 4-6 biscuits on each sheet. Bake for 10-12 minutes, until the tops are cracked and shiny; do not overbake or they will break when removed from the baking sheet.

◆ Remove the baking sheets to a wire rack to cool until the biscuits are firm, but not too crisp. Before they become too crisp, transfer each biscuit to a wire rack to cool completely. Continue to bake in batches. Store the biscuits in an airtight container.

SWEET SUCCESS

If you need to use the same baking sheets to bake in batches, cool by running the back of the baking sheet under cold water and wiping the surface with a paper towel before regreasing.

Chocolate Amaretti Biscuits

MAKES ABOUT 24

150 g (5 oz) blanched whole almonds
100 g (4 oz) caster sugar
1 tbsp cocoa powder
2 tbsp icing sugar
2 egg whites
pinch of cream of tartar
1 tsp almond essence
icing sugar for dusting

◆ Preheat the oven to 180°C (350°F, Gas Mark 4). Place the almonds on a small baking sheet and bake for 10-12 minutes, stirring occasionally, until golden brown. Remove from the oven and cool to room temperature; reduce the oven temperature to 170°C (325°F, Gas Mark 3). Line a large baking sheet with greaseproof paper or foil.

◆ In a food processor fitted with the metal blade, process the almonds with 50 g (2 oz) sugar until the almonds are finely ground, but not oily. Transfer to a bowl and sift in the cocoa powder and icing sugar; stir to blend. Set aside.

◆ With an electric mixer, beat the egg whites and cream of tartar until soft peaks form. Sprinkle in the remaining sugar, 1 tbsp at a time, beating well after each addition, until the whites are glossy and stiff. Beat in the almond essence.

◆ Sprinkle the almond sugar mixture over and gently fold into the beaten whites just until blended. Spoon the mixture into a large piping bag fitted with a plain 1 cm (½ inch) nozzle. Pipe 4 cm (1½ inch) circles about 2.5 cm (1 inch) apart on to the prepared baking sheet.

◆ Bake for 12-15 minutes, or until the biscuits appear crisp. Transfer the baking sheets to a wire rack to cool for 10 minutes. With a palette knife, transfer the biscuits to a wire rack to cool completely. When cool, dust with icing sugar and store in an airtight container.

VARIATION

As an alternative decoration, lightly press a few coffee-sugar crystals onto top of each biscuit before baking.

Chocolate Chip Cookies

MAKES ABOUT 30

100 g (4 oz) self-raising flour
25 g (1 oz) unsweetened cocoa powder
½ tsp baking powder
100 g (4 oz) butter or margarine
75 g (3 oz) brown sugar
50 g (2 oz) sugar
2 eggs
2.5 ml (½ tsp) vanilla essence
175 g (6 oz) chocolate chips
75 g (3 oz) chopped walnuts

◆ Preheat the oven to 190°C (375°F, Gas Mark 5). Sieve together the flour, cocoa and baking powder.

◆ Beat together the butter or margarine and sugars until light and fluffy.

◆ Beat in the eggs one at a time. Add the vanilla essence.

◆ Add the dry ingredients and beat until well combined.

◆ Stir in the chocolate chips and nuts.

◆ Drop the dough in heaped teaspoonfuls on to a baking sheet. Bake in the oven for about 10 minutes.

◆ Cool for a minute then remove from the baking sheet and cool on a wire rack.

Bittersweet Fudge Biscuits

MAKES ABOUT 36

175 g (6 oz) bittersweet chocolate, chopped
100g (4 oz) unsalted butter, at room temperature
100 g (4 oz) sugar
2 eggs
5 ml (1 tsp) vanilla essence
175 g (6 oz) plain flour
½ tsp salt
90 g (3½ oz) pecans, chopped and toasted
75 g (3 oz) good-quality white chocolate, chopped into 5 mm (¼ inch) pieces
melted chocolate, to decorate

◆ In the top of a double boiler over low heat, melt the chocolate, stirring frequently until smooth. Remove from the heat.

◆ With an electric mixer, cream the butter, sugar, eggs and vanilla essence until creamy and smooth, 2-3 minutes, scraping the bowl occasionally. Slowly beat in the cooled chocolate until well blended.

◆ Gradually stir in the flour and salt, stirring just until blended. Stir in the pecans and chopped white chocolate. Cover the bowl with clingfilm and refrigerate for 1 hour or until firm.

◆ Meanwhile, preheat the oven to 190°C/375°F/Gas Mark 5. Lightly grease 2 large baking sheets. Drop rounded teaspoonfuls of dough at least 5 cm (2 inches) apart on to the prepared baking sheets, flattening slightly. You may need to cook them in 2 batches.

◆ Bake for 8-10 minutes, or just until the surface feels slightly firm when touched with a fingertip. Remove the baking sheets to wire racks to cool for 5-7 minutes. With a palette knife, remove the biscuits to a wire rack to cool completely. Repeat with the remaining dough. When cool, drizzle chocolate over them using a spoon. Store in airtight containers.

Chocolate Pinwheels

MAKES ABOUT 40

175 g (6 oz) butter or margarine
175 g (6 oz) sugar
1 large egg, beaten
1 tsp vanilla essence
350 g (12 oz) self-raising flour
3 tbsp unsweetened cocoa powder
a little beaten egg white

◆ Put the butter or margarine and sugar into a bowl and cream together until light and fluffy.
◆ Beat in the egg and vanilla essence.
◆ Work the flour into the creamed mixture.
◆ Divide the mixture in half and knead the cocoa into one half. Shape into 2 smooth balls. Wrap in clingfilm and chill.

◆ To make pinwheel biscuits, roll out the plain and chocolate doughs separately into equal rectangles. Brush the plain dough with egg white and place the chocolate mixture on top. Brush the chocolate mixture with egg white.
◆ Roll up like a Swiss roll. Wrap in foil and chill.
◆ Cut into 5 mm (¼ inch) thick slices. Place on a baking sheet and bake in a preheated oven at 190°C (375°F, Gas Mark 5) for about 8 minutes.

VARIATIONS

◆ To make chequerboard biscuits, reserve about a quarter of the plain dough.
◆ Shape the remaining plain and chocolate doughs each into 2 long thin rolls. Brush with egg white.
◆ Put a chocolate roll next to a plain roll. Place the other 2 rolls on top, reversing the colours. Press lightly together.

◆ Roll out the reserved plain dough to a large rectangle. Brush with egg white and roll it around the 4 thin rolls. Chill, slice and cook as in recipe above.
◆ To make owl biscuits, roll out the plain mixture to a rectangle.
◆ Form the chocolate mixture into a roll. Brush with egg white and roll up in the plain mixture.
◆ Wrap and chill.
◆ Cut into 5 mm (¼ inch) slices.
◆ To form the owl's head, put 2 circles side by side. Brush the join with egg white and press lightly together.
◆ Pinch the top corners of each head to form ears.
◆ Place almonds halves in the centre of each head for the beak. Put 2 chocolate dots for the eyes.
◆ Cook as in the main recipe.

Chocolate-Mint Sandwich Biscuits

MAKES ABOUT 20

100 g (4 oz) unsalted butter, softened
50 g (2 oz) sugar
1 egg
100 g (4 oz) butter or margarine
5 ml (1 tsp) peppermint essence
25 g (1 oz) cocoa powder
100 g (4 oz) plain flour

White chocolate ganache filling
120 ml (4 fl oz) whipping cream
175 g (6 oz) good-quality white chocolate, chopped
5 ml (1 tsp) peppermint essence
150 g (5 oz) plain chocolate, chopped
40 g (1½ oz) unsalted butter

◆ With an electric mixer, beat the butter and sugar until light and creamy, about 3 minutes. Add the egg and beat for 2–3 minutes longer, until the mixture is fluffy. Beat in the peppermint essence.
◆ Sift the cocoa and flour together into a bowl. With a wooden spoon, gradually stir into the creamy butter mixture just until blended. Turn out the dough on to a piece of clingfilm and use to flatten the dough to a thick disc. Wrap and refrigerate for 1 hour.
◆ Preheat the oven to 180°C (350°F, Gas Mark 4). Grease and flour 2 large baking sheets. Remove the dough from the refrigerator and divide in half. Refrigerate one half of dough.
◆ On a lightly floured surface, roll out the other half of the dough to about 3 mm (⅛ inch) thick. Using a floured heart-shaped or flower-shaped cutter, about 5 cm (2 inches) in diameter, cut out as many shapes as possible and place the shapes on prepared baking sheets; reserve any trimmings. Repeat with the second half of the dough.
◆ Bake for 7–8 minutes, until the edges are set; do not overbake as biscuits burn easily. Transfer the baking sheets to a wire rack to cool for 10 minutes. With a palette knife, transfer the biscuits to a wire rack to cool completely.
◆ Prepare the filling. In a saucepan over medium heat, bring the cream to the boil. Remove from the heat. Add the white chocolate all at once, stirring constantly until smooth. Stir in the peppermint essence and pour into a bowl. Cool for about 1 hour until firm but not hard.
◆ With a hand-held electric mixer, beat the white chocolate filling for 30–45 seconds, until it becomes lighter and fluffier. Spread a little white chocolate filling on to the bottom of 1 biscuit and immediately cover it with another biscuit, pressing together gently. Repeat with the remaining biscuits and filling. Refrigerate for 30 minutes, or until firm.
◆ In a saucepan over low heat, melt the chocolate and butter, stirring frequently until smooth. Remove from the heat. Cool for 15 minutes until slightly thickened.
◆ Spread a small amount of glaze on to the top of each sandwiched biscuit, being careful not to let the glaze drip or spread over the edges. Chill until the glaze is set.

RIGHT *Chocolate-Mint Sandwich Biscuits*

Florentines

MAKES ABOUT 8-10

50 g (2 oz) butter
50 g (2 oz) sugar
25 g (1 oz) plain flour, sieved
50 g (2 oz) almonds, blanched and chopped
50 g (2 oz) candied peel, chopped
25 g (1 oz) raisins, chopped
25 g (1 oz) glacé cherries, washed and chopped
rind of ½ lemon, finely grated
100 g (4 oz) plain chocolate

◆ Preheat the oven to 180°C (350°F, Gas Mark 4). Line baking sheets with greaseproof paper.
◆ Put the butter and sugar into a pan and gently heat them together until melted.
◆ Remove the pan from the heat and stir in the flour.
◆ Add the almonds, candied peel, raisins, cherries and lemon rind. Stir well.
◆ Put teaspoonfuls of the mixture well apart on the baking sheets.
◆ Bake in the oven for about 10 minutes or until golden brown.
◆ While still warm, press the edges of the biscuits back to a neat shape. Leave to cool on the baking sheets until set, then carefully lift on to a wire rack.
◆ Melt the chocolate. Spread over the smooth sides of the florentines. As the chocolate begins to set, mark into wavy lines with a fork. Leave to set.

Triple Decker Squares

MAKES 16

100 g (4 oz) butter or margarine
50 g (2 oz) sugar
175 g (6 oz) plain flour

Filling
100 g (4 oz) butter or margarine
75 g (3 oz) sugar
2 tbsp golden syrup
196 g (6 oz) can condensed milk

Topping
175 g (6 oz) plain chocolate
30 ml (2 tbsp) milk

◆ Preheat the oven to 180°C (350°F, Gas Mark 4). Cream together the butter or margarine and sugar until light and fluffy.
◆ Stir in the flour. Work the dough with your hands and knead well together.
◆ Roll out and press into a shallow 20 cm (8 inch) square pan. Prick well with a fork.
◆ Bake in the oven for 25-30 minutes. Cool in the pan.
◆ To make the filling, put all the ingredients into a pan and heat gently, stirring until the sugar has dissolved. Bring to the boil and cook, stirring for 5-7 minutes until golden.

◆ Pour the caramel over the shortbread base and leave to set.
◆ Melt the chocolate and milk together. Spread it evenly over the caramel. Leave until quite cold before cutting into squares.

Viennese Chocolate Biscuits

MAKES ABOUT 20

225 g (8 oz) butter or margarine
50 g (2 oz) icing sugar, sieved
225 g (8 oz) plain flour
50 g (2 oz) drinking chocolate powder
25 g (1 oz) cornflour
100 g (4 oz) plain chocolate
a little icing sugar

◆ Preheat the oven to 180°C (350°F, Gas Mark 4). Cream together the butter or margarine and sugar until light and fluffy.
◆ Work in the flour, drinking chocolate powder and cornflour.
◆ Put the mixture into a piping bag fitted with a large star nozzle. Pipe in fingers, or shells, or "s" shapes on to greased baking sheets.
◆ Bake in the oven for 20-25 minutes. Cool on a wire rack.
◆ Melt the chocolate. Dip half of each biscuit into the chocolate and leave to set on greaseproof paper.
◆ Dust the uncoated halves of the biscuits with icing sugar.

VARIATION

To make chocolate gems, pipe mixture into small individual star shapes. Bake for about half the time. Place a chocolate button in the centre of each one while still hot.

MALL CAKES

Raspberry Chocolate Eclairs

MAKES ABOUT 10

50 g (2 oz) butter or margarine,
cut in pieces
150 ml (¼ pt) water
65 g (2½ oz) plain flour
2 eggs, beaten

Filling
150 ml (¼ pt) double (table) cream
225 g (8 oz) fresh raspberries
a little sugar

Topping
175 g (6 oz) plain chocolate
25 g (1 oz) butter

◆ Preheat the oven to 200°C (400°F, Gas Mark 6). Put the butter or margarine and water into a pan and bring to the boil.

◆ Remove from the heat and tip all the flour into the pan at once. Beat with a wooden spoon until the paste forms a ball. Cool.

◆ Whisk the eggs into the paste, a little at a time. Continue beating until the mixture is glossy.

◆ Put the pastry into a piping bag fitted with a large plain nozzle. Pipe 7.5 cm (3 inch) lengths on to greased baking sheets.

◆ Bake in the oven for about 25 minutes, until golden brown.

◆ Remove from the oven and make a couple of slits in the sides of each one to allow steam to escape. Return to the oven for a few minutes to dry. Cool on a wire rack.

◆ To make the filling, whisk the cream until stiff. Fold in the raspberries and sugar to taste.

◆ Make a slit down the side of each eclair and fill with the cream mixture.

◆ Melt together the chocolate and butter. Dip the tops of the eclairs into the chocolate and then leave to set.

Chocolate-Mint Cup Cakes

MAKES ABOUT 18-20

225 g (8 oz) plain flour
1 tsp bicarbonate of soda
¼ tsp salt
50 g (2 oz) cocoa powder
150 g (5 oz) butter, softened
275 g (10 oz) caster sugar
3 eggs
10 ml (2 tsp) peppermint essence
225 ml (8 fl oz) milk

Chocolate-mint glaze
75 g (3 oz) plain chocolate
50 g (2 oz) butter
5 ml (1 tsp) peppermint essence

◆ Preheat the oven to 180°C (350°F, Gas Mark 4). Line 20 deep muffin or bun tins with paper cases.
◆ Sift together the flour, bicarbonate of soda, salt and cocoa powder.
◆ In a second large bowl, using an electric mixer, beat the butter and sugar until light and creamy, about 5 minutes. Add the eggs, 1 at a time, beating well after each addition, then beat in the mint essence.
◆ On low speed, beat in the flour and cocoa mixture alternately with the milk just until blended. Spoon into paper cases, filling each tin about three-quarters full.

◆ Bake for 12-15 minutes, until a fine skewer inserted in the centre comes out clean; do not overbake. Cool in the tins on a wire rack for 5 minutes; remove the cakes to wire rack to cool completely.
◆ Meanwhile, prepare the glaze. In a saucepan over low heat, melt the chocolate and butter, stirring until smooth. Remove from the heat and stir in the mint essence. Cool until spreadable, then spread on top of each cake.

RIGHT *Chocolate-Mint Cup Cakes*

Chocolate Meringues

MAKES 6-8

3 egg whites
75 g (3 oz) caster sugar
75 g (3 oz) icing sugar, sieved
25 g (1 oz) unsweetened cocoa powder, sieved

Filling
150 ml (¼ pt) double cream
1 tbsp soft brown sugar
2 tsp unsweetened cocoa powder

◆ Preheat the oven to 110°C (225°F, Gas Mark ¼). Beat the egg whites until they form stiff peaks. Gradually whisk in the caster sugar, a little at a time.
◆ Whisk in the icing sugar.
◆ Fold in the cocoa powder.
◆ Put the mixture into a piping bag fitted with a large star nozzle. Line baking sheets with greaseproof paper.
◆ Pipe the mixture into spirals.

◆ Bake in the oven for 2-3 hours or until the meringues are dry. Cool on a wire rack.
◆ Whip the cream until stiff. Stir in the sugar and cocoa. Sandwich the meringues together, two at a time, with the chocolate cream.

Cream Cheese-Marbled Brownies

SERVES 15-20

250 g (9 oz) bittersweet chocolate, chopped
225 g (8 oz) unsalted butter, softened
225 g (8 oz) granulated sugar
50 g (2 oz) soft brown sugar
3 eggs
15 ml (1 tbsp) vanilla essence
100 g (4 oz) plain flour
¼ tsp salt
450 g (1 lb) cream cheese, softened
1 egg
5 ml (1 tsp) vanilla essence
finely grated zest of 1 lemon

◆ Preheat the oven to 180°C (350°F, Gas Mark 4). Invert a 23 x 32.5 cm (9 x 13 inch) baking tin and mould foil over the bottom. Turn the tin over and line with the foil; leave the foil to extend above the sides of the tin. Grease the bottom and sides of the foil.

◆ In a saucepan over low heat, melt the chocolate and 100 g (4 oz) of the butter, stirring frequently until smooth. Remove from the heat. Cool to room temperature.

◆ In a bowl, using a hand-held mixer, beat the remaining butter, 150 g (5 oz) granulated sugar and the brown sugar until light and creamy, 2-3 minutes. Add the eggs, 1 at a time, beating well after each addition. Beat in the vanilla essence, then slowly beat in the melted chocolate and butter. Stir in the flour and salt just until blended.

◆ In a bowl, using a hand-held electric mixer, beat the cream cheese and remaining sugar until smooth, about 1 minute. Beat in the egg, vanilla essence and lemon zest.

◆ Pour two-thirds of the brownie batter into the tin and spread evenly. Pour the cream cheese mixture over the brownie layer. Spoon the remaining brownie mixture in dollops on top of the cream cheese mixture in 2 rows along the long side of the tin. Using a knife or spoon, swirl the brownie batter into the cream cheese batter to create a marble effect.

◆ Bake for 25-35 minutes, or until a cocktail stick or fine skewer inserted 5 cm (2 inches) from the edge of the tin comes out with just a few crumbs attached. Transfer to a wire rack to cool in the tin.

◆ When cool, use the foil to help lift the brownie out of the tin. Invert on to another rack or baking sheet and peel off the foil. Invert back on to the wire rack and slide on to a serving plate. Cut into squares and wrap and refrigerate; or wrap until ready to serve, then cut into squares.

Chocolate and Coconut Sarah Bernhardts

MAKES ABOUT 16

90 g (3½ oz) shredded coconut
75 g (3 oz) sugar
2 tbsp plain flour
3 tbsp cocoa powder
1 tsp vanilla essence
1 tbsp golden syrup
2-3 egg whites

Ganache topping
175 ml (6 fl oz) cream
225 g (8 oz) plain chocolate, chopped
25 g (1 oz) pieces unsalted butter
2 tbsp shredded coconut

Chocolate glaze
175 g (6 oz) plain chocolate, chopped
25 g (1 oz) pieces unsalted butter
1 tbsp golden syrup

◆ First prepare the topping. In a medium saucepan over medium heat, bring the cream to the boil. Remove from the heat. Add the chocolate all at once, stirring well until melted and smooth. Beat in the butter. Cool, then refrigerate for 1-2 hours, until thickened and chilled, but not set.

◆ Preheat the oven to 170°C (325°F, Gas Mark 3). Line a large baking sheet with foil and grease the foil. In a bowl, combine the coconut, sugar, flour and cocoa powder. Stir in the vanilla and golden syrup and 2 egg whites; if the mixture is too dry, add the third egg white, little by little, until a thick dough-like batter forms and holds together.

◆ Using a miniature ice cream scoop, about 2.5 cm (1 inch) in diameter, or a teaspoon, place 16 scoops on to the baking sheet. With your index finger, flatten each scoop, making a slight indentation in the centre of each.

◆ Bake for 12-14 minutes, just until the macaroons are set on the outside. Do not overbake or they will be too hard. Cool on the baking sheet for 10-15 minutes, then remove from the foil to a wire rack to cool completely.

◆ When the topping mixture is cold and thick, beat with an electric mixer for 30-45 seconds, just until the mixture lightens in colour and thickens enough to pipe; do not overbeat or the mixture will become grainy.

◆ Quickly spoon the mixture into a large piping bag fitted with a 1 cm (½ inch) plain nozzle and pipe a 2.5 cm (1 inch) mound on top of each macaroon, pressing the tip firmly on to the centre. Chill for 1-2 hours, until the topping is firm.

◆ Prepare the glaze. In a small saucepan over a low heat, melt the chocolate and butter with golden syrup, stirring frequently until smooth. Pour into a tall, narrow container, mug or strong paper cup to allow for easy dipping. Cool the chocolate.

◆ Holding each macaroon by the very bottom edge, carefully and quickly dip into the chocolate glaze to cover the filling and top of each macaroon to within about 5 mm (¼ inch) of the bottom, twisting and swirling in chocolate glaze so the entire macaroon is coated. Leave the excess to drip off, then quickly turn upright and place on a baking sheet. Decorate the tops with a sprinkling of coconut.

Chunky Chocolate Brownies with Fudge Glaze

MAKES 14–16

275 g (10 oz) bittersweet chocolate, chopped
50 g (2 oz) unsalted butter, cut into pieces
75 g (3 oz) brown sugar
50 g (2 oz) granulated sugar
2 eggs
15 ml (1 tbsp) vanilla essence
50 g (2 oz) plain flour
90 g (3½ oz) pecans or walnuts, chopped and toasted
150 g (5 oz) good-quality white chocolate, chopped into 5 mm (¼ inch) pieces

Fudgy chocolate glaze
175 g (6 oz) plain chocolate, chopped
50 g (2 oz) unsalted butter, cut into pieces
2 tbsp golden syrup
10 ml (2 tsp) vanilla essence
1 tsp instant coffee powder

◆ Preheat the oven to 180°C (350°F, Gas Mark 4). Invert a 20 cm (8 inch) square baking tin and mould a piece of foil over the bottom. Turn the tin over and line with the moulded foil. Lightly grease foil.

◆ In a saucepan over low heat, melt the chocolate and butter, stirring frequently until smooth. Remove the pan from the heat.

◆ Stir in the sugars and continue stirring for 2 minutes longer, until the sugar is dissolved. Beat in the eggs and vanilla essence. Stir in the flour until blended. Stir in the nuts and chopped chocolate. Pour into the lined tin.

◆ Bake for 20-25 minutes, until a cocktail stick or fine skewer inserted 5 cm (2 inches) from the centre comes out with just a few crumbs attached; do not overbake. Transfer to a wire rack to cool for 30 minutes. Using the foil as a guide, remove the brownie from the tin and cool on the rack for at least 2 hours.

◆ Prepare the glaze. In a saucepan over medium heat, melt the chocolate, butter, golden syrup, vanilla essence and coffee powder, stirring frequently until smooth. Remove from the heat. Refrigerate for 1 hour, or until thickened and spreadable.

◆ Invert the brownie on to a plate and remove the foil. Invert back on to the rack and slide on to a serving plate, top-side up. Using a palette knife, spread a thick layer of glaze over the top of the brownie just to the edges. Refrigerate for 1 hour, until set. Cut into squares or bars.

Jaffa Cakes

MAKES 18

2 eggs
50 g (2 oz) sugar
65 g (2½ oz) self-raising flour, sieved
approximately 4 tbsp marmalade,
sieved
100 g (4 oz) plain chocolate
zest of ¼ orange, finely grated
10 ml (2 tsp) corn oil
15 ml (1 tbsp) water

◆ Preheat the oven to 200°C (400°F, Gas Mark 6). Put the eggs and sugar into a bowl. Whisk until thick and creamy so that when the whisk is lifted the mixture leaves a trail. If using a hand whisk, put the bowl over a pan of hot water.
◆ With a metal spoon, fold in the flour.
◆ Spoon the mixture into about 18 well-greased, round-bottomed patty tins. Bake for about 10 minutes until golden brown.
◆ Remove and cool on a wire rack.
◆ Spread a little marmalade over each cake.

◆ Put the chocolate, orange zest, oil and water into a bowl over a pan of hot water. Stir well until melted. Cool until the chocolate starts to thicken and then spoon over the marmalade. Leave to set.

Butterfly Cakes

MAKES 14-16

100 g (4 oz) butter or margarine
100 g (4 oz) sugar
2 eggs
5 ml (1 tsp) grated orange zest
50 g (2 oz) plain chocolate, finely grated
100 g (4 oz) self-raising flour

Icing
75 g (3 oz) butter or margarine
175g (6 oz) icing sugar, sieved
75 g (3 oz) plain chocolate, melted

To decorate
icing sugar
seedless raspberry jam or glacé cherries

◆ Preheat the oven to 180°C (350°F, Gas Mark 4). Put the butter or margarine and sugar into a bowl and cream together until light and fluffy.
◆ Beat in the eggs a little at a time. Stir in the orange zest and chocolate.
◆ Fold in the flour.
◆ Arrange paper cases in a metal bun tin. Divide the mixture between the cases.
◆ Bake in the oven for about 15-20 minutes. Cool.
◆ To make the icing, cream together the butter and icing sugar. Gradually beat in the cooled, melted chocolate.
◆ Starting 5 mm (¼ inch) in from the edge, remove the top of each cake by cutting in and slightly down to form a cavity.

◆ Pipe a little icing in the cavity of each cake.
◆ Sprinkle the reserved cake tops with icing sugar and cut each one in half. Place each half, cut side outwards, on to the icing to form wings.
◆ Pipe small rosettes of icing in the centre of each cake. Top with a small blob of raspberry jam or half a glacé cherry.

Cocoa Brownies with Milk Chocolate and Walnut Topping

SERVES 12

50 g (2 oz) plain flour
40 g (1½ oz) cocoa powder
¼ tsp baking powder
¼ tsp salt
100 g (4 oz) unsalted butter
225 g (8 oz) sugar
2 eggs
10 ml (2 tsp) vanilla essence
75 g (3 oz) walnuts, coarsely chopped

Milk chocolate and walnut topping
175-200 g (6-7 oz) milk chocolate
75 g (3 oz) walnuts, chopped

◆ Preheat the oven to 180°C (350°F, Gas Mark 4). Grease a 23 cm (9 inch) springform tin or 23 cm (9 inch) cake tin with a removable bottom. Into a bowl sift the flour, cocoa powder, baking powder and salt. Set aside.

◆ In a medium saucepan over medium heat, melt the butter. Stir in the sugar and remove from the heat, stirring 2-3 minutes to dissolve the sugar. Beat in the eggs and vanilla essence. Stir in the flour mixture just until blended; then stir in the walnuts. Pour into the prepared tin, smoothing the top evenly.

◆ Bake for 18-24 minutes, until a cocktail stick or fine skewer inserted 5 cm (2 inches) from the centre comes out with just a few crumbs attached; do not overbake or the brownie will be dry.

◆ Prepare the topping. Break the milk chocolate into pieces. As soon as the brownie tests done, remove from the oven to a heatproof surface. Quickly place the chocolate pieces all over the top of the brownie; do not let the chocolate touch the side of the tin. Return to the oven for 20-30 seconds.

◆ Remove the brownie and, with the back of a spoon, gently spread the softened chocolate evenly over the top. Sprinkle walnuts evenly over the top and, with the back of a spoon, gently press them into the chocolate. Cool on a wire rack for 30 minutes.

◆ Refrigerate for 1 hour, until set. Run a knife around the edge of the tin to loosen the brownie from the edge. Carefully remove the side of the tin. Cool completely and serve at room temperature.

RIGHT *Cocoa Brownies with Milk Chocolate and Walnut Topping*

Classic Brownies

MAKES ABOUT 20

225 g (8 oz) soft brown sugar
50 g (2 oz) unsweetened cocoa powder, sieved
75 g (3 oz) self-raising flour
2 eggs
30 ml (2 tbsp) milk
100 g (4 oz) butter, melted
50 g (2 oz) walnuts, finely chopped
50 g (2 oz) raisins, chopped
walnut halves, to decorate

Icing
100 g (4 oz) plain chocolate
1 tbsp black coffee

◆ Preheat the oven to 180°C (350°F, Gas Mark 4). Mix together the sugar, cocoa and flour.

◆ Beat together the eggs and milk. Stir into the flour mixture, together with the butter, walnuts and raisins.

◆ Spread in a greased and base-lined pan measuring 18 x 28 x 4 cm (7 x 11 x 1½ inches).

◆ Bake in the oven for about 30 minutes. Cool.

◆ Melt the chocolate and coffee together. Spread over the cake.

◆ To serve, decorate with walnut halves. Cut into squares when cold.

Chocolate Boxes

1 egg
25 g (1 oz) sugar
25 g (1 oz) plain flour

Filling
150 ml (¼ pt) water
150 g (5 oz) pkt tangerine jelly
225 g (8 oz) curd cheese
300 ml (½ pt) double cream
2 tbsp apricot jam, sieved

To decorate
36 x 5 cm (2 inch) chocolate squares
(see page 18)
whipped cream
9 mandarin orange segments
quartered walnuts

RIGHT *Chocolate Boxes*

◆ Preheat the oven to 200°C (400°F, Gas Mark 6). Whisk the egg and sugar together until the mixture is thick and creamy and the whisk leaves a trail when lifted.
◆ Using a metal spoon, gently fold in the flour. Pour into a shallow greased and base-lined 18 cm (7 inch) square tin.
◆ Bake for 10-12 minutes. Turn out and cool.
◆ Heat the water. Add the jelly and stir until dissolved. Chill until the mixture begins to turn syrupy.
◆ Beat the cheese and gradually add the jelly.
◆ Whip the cream until thick and fold into the cheese mixture. Pour into an 18 cm (7 inch) square cake tin, lined with greaseproof paper. Chill until set.

◆ Spread the sponge with apricot jam. Unmould the cheese mixture on to the sponge. Trim the edges.
◆ Cut the cake into nine squares. Press a chocolate square on to each side of each cake.
◆ To serve, pipe whipped cream on top of each chocolate box. Top with mandarins and walnuts.

Variations
◆ Use cherry jelly, cherry jam and top with canned or fresh cherries.
◆ Use strawberry/raspberry jelly, strawberry/raspberry jam and top with fresh strawberries/raspberries.
◆ Use lemon jelly, lemon curd and top with pieces of canned or fresh pineapple.
◆ Use lime jelly, lime marmalade and top with halved slices of kiwi fruit.

Chocolate Malties

75 g (3 oz) plain chocolate
75 g (3 oz) cream cheese
50 g (2 oz) butter or margarine
25 g (1 oz) instant malted milk
powder
2.5 ml (½ tsp) vanilla essence
375 g (12 oz) icing sugar, sieved
90 ml (3½ fl oz) milk
200g (7 oz) self-raising flour
½ tsp baking powder
25 g (1 oz) softened butter or
margarine
2 eggs
45 ml (3 tbsp) milk
chocolate buttons, to decorate

◆ Preheat the oven to 180°C (350°F, Gas Mark 4). Melt the chocolate and allow to cool slightly.

◆ Beat together the cream cheese, butter or margarine, malted milk powder and vanilla essence.
◆ Beat in the icing sugar and half the milk alternately. Beat in the melted chocolate.
◆ Remove 225 g (8 oz) of the chocolate mixture. Cover and reserve for the icing.
◆ Sieve together the flour and baking powder.
◆ Beat the softened butter into the chocolate mixture.
◆ Beat in the eggs.
◆ Stir in the flour alternately with the remaining milk.
◆ Put paper cases into patty tins and fill two-thirds full with the mixture.
◆ Bake in the oven for about 20 minutes. Cool.

◆ To serve, ice the cakes with the reserved chocolate icing. Decorate with chocolate buttons if you wish.

LARGE CAKES and GATEAUX

Triple Chocolate Cheesecake

SERVES 18-20

225 g (8 oz) plain chocolate digestive
biscuits
50 g (2 oz) butter, melted
½ tsp ground cinnamon

Filling
450 g (1 lb) plain chocolate, chopped
50 g (2 oz) butter, cut into pieces
250 ml (8 fl oz) soured cream
900 g (2 lb) cream cheese, softened
225 g (8 oz) sugar
5 eggs
15 ml (1 tbsp) vanilla essence

Chocolate glaze
100 g (4 oz) plain chocolate, chopped
120 ml (4 fl oz) double cream
5 ml (1 tsp) vanilla essence
cocoa powder

◆ Preheat the oven to 180°C (350°F, Gas Mark 4). Lightly grease the bottom and sides of a 25 cm (10 inch), 7.5 cm (3 inch) deep springform tin.

◆ Prepare the crust. In a food processor, process the chocolate biscuits until fine crumbs form. Pour in the melted butter and cinnamon. Process just until blended. Pat onto the bottom and to within 1 cm (½ inch) of the top of the sides of the tin.

◆ Bake for 5-7 minutes, just until set. Remove to a wire rack to cool while you prepare the filling. Lower the oven temperature to 170°C (325°F, Gas Mark 3).

◆ Prepare the filling. In a saucepan over low heat, melt the chocolate and butter, stirring frequently until smooth. Set aside to cool; stir in the soured cream.

◆ With an electric mixer, beat the cream cheese and sugar until smooth, 2-4 minutes. Add the eggs, 1 at a time, beating well after each addition, scraping the bowl occasionally. Slowly beat in the chocolate mixture and vanilla essence just until blended. Pour into the baked crust. Place the tin on a baking sheet; place a small saucepan of water on the floor of the oven to create moisture.

◆ Bake for 1-1½ hours, or until the edge of the cheesecake is set but the centre is still slightly soft. Turn off the oven but leave the cheesecake in the oven for another 30 minutes. Remove to a wire rack to cool. Run a knife around the edge of the cheesecake in the tin to separate it from the side; this helps to prevent cracking. Cool to room temperature.

◆ Prepare the glaze. In a saucepan, melt the chocolate with the cream and vanilla essence, stirring until smooth. Cool and leave to thicken slightly, 10-15 minutes. Pour over the warm cake in the tin; cool the glazed cake completely. Using strips of greaseproof paper dust cocoa in horizontal bands across the top of the cake. Refrigerate, loosely covered, overnight.

◆ To serve, run a knife around the edge of the tin to loosen the cheesecake. Remove the side of the tin. If you like, slide a knife under the crust to separate the cheesecake from the base, and, with a palette knife, slide it on to a serving plate.

Chocolate and Banana Swirl Cheesecake

SERVES 16

Crumb crust
150 g (5 oz) ginger snaps
40 g (1½ oz) walnuts
50 g (2 oz) butter, melted
½ tsp ground ginger

Filling
100 g (4 oz) plain chocolate, chopped
50 g (2 oz) butter, cut into pieces
1 kg (2½ lb) cream cheese, softened
275 g (10 oz) sugar
15 ml (1 tbsp) vanilla essence
5 eggs
250 ml (8 fl oz) soured cream
3 ripe bananas
15 ml (1 tbsp) lemon juice

◆ Preheat the oven to 180°C (350°F, Gas Mark 4). Lightly grease a 25 cm (10 inch), 7.5 cm (3 inch) deep springform tin.

◆ In a food processor, process the ginger snaps and walnuts until fine crumbs form. Pour in the melted butter and ginger. Process just until blended. Pat onto the bottom and to within 1 cm (½ inch) of the top of the sides of the tin.

◆ Bake for 5-7 minutes, just until set. Remove to a wire rack to cool while preparing the filling. Lower the oven temperature to 150°C (300°F, Gas Mark 2).

◆ In a saucepan over a low heat, melt the chocolate and butter, stirring frequently until smooth. Set aside to cool.

◆ With an electric mixer, beat the cream cheese and sugar until smooth, 2-4 minutes; stir in the vanilla essence. Add the eggs, 1 at a time, beating well after each addition, scraping the bowl occasionally, then blend in the soured cream. Pour about 350 ml (12 fl oz) of cream cheese mixture into a bowl and stir in the melted chocolate until well blended. Set the mixture aside.

◆ In a second bowl, mash the bananas with the lemon juice, then beat into the remaining cream cheese mixture until well blended.

◆ Pour the banana mixture into the baked crust. Drop spoonfuls of chocolate mixture over the banana mixture in a circle about 2.5 cm (1 inch) from the sides of the tin. With a spoon or knife, swirl the chocolate mixture into the banana

mixture, creating a marbled effect. Do not overmix. Place the tin on a baking sheet; place a small saucepan of water on the floor of the oven to create moisture during baking.

◆ Bake for 50-60 minutes, until the edge of the cheesecake is set, but the centre is still soft. Turn off the oven and leave to stand for 30 minutes; this helps to prevent cracking. Transfer to a wire rack, run a knife around the edge of the cheesecake in the tin to separate it from the sides; this also helps to prevent cracking. Cool completely, then refrigerate, loosely covered, overnight.

◆ To serve, run a knife around the edge of the tin to loosen the cheesecake. Remove the side of the tin. If you like, slide a knife under the crust to separate the cheesecake from the base, then, with a palette knife, slide on to a serving plate. Alternatively, leave the cheesecake on the tin base to avoid breaking the crust or surface and serve from the tin base.

White Chocolate Cheesecake

SERVES 16-20

Crumb crust
150 g (5 oz) digestive biscuits
25 g (1 oz) pecan or walnut halves
50 g (2 oz) butter, melted
2.5 ml (½ tsp) ground cinnamon

Filling
350 g (12 oz) good-quality white
chocolate, chopped
120 ml (4 fl oz) whipping cream
675 g (1½ lb) cream cheese
75 g (3 oz) sugar
4 eggs
15 ml (1 tbsp) vanilla essence

To decorate
cocoa powder for dusting (optional)
white and dark chocolate curls (see
page 18)

Soured cream topping
400 ml (14 fl oz) soured cream
50 g (2 oz) sugar
5 ml (1 tsp) vanilla essence

◆ Preheat the oven to 180°C (350°F, Gas Mark4). Lightly grease a 23 cm (9 inch), 7.5 cm (3 inch) deep springform tin.

◆ Prepare the crust. In a food processor, process the biscuits and nuts until fine crumbs form. Pour in the melted butter and cinnamon. Process just until blended. Pat on to the bottom and to within 1 cm (½ inch) of the top of the sides of the tin.

◆ Bake for 5-7 minutes, just until set. Remove to a wire rack to cool while you prepare the filling. Lower the oven temperature to 150°C (300°F, Gas Mark 2).

◆ Prepare the filling. In a saucepan over a low heat, melt the chocolate with the cream, stirring frequently until smooth. Set aside to cool.

◆ With an electric mixer, beat the cream cheese and sugar until smooth, 2-4 minutes. Add the eggs, 1 at a time, beating well after each addition, scraping the bowl occasionally. Slowly beat in the white chocolate mixture and vanilla essence just until blended. Pour into the baked crust. Place on a baking sheet; place a small saucepan of water on the floor of the oven to create moisture during baking.

◆ Bake for 45-55 minutes, or until the edge of the cheesecake is firm but the centre is still slightly soft. Remove the cheesecake to a wire rack. Increase the oven temperature to 200°C (400°F, Gas Mark 6).

◆ Prepare the topping. In a bowl, beat the soured cream, sugar and vanilla essence. Pour over the cheesecake and return to the oven. Bake for 5 minutes longer. Transfer to a wire rack to cool to room temperature. Run a knife around the edge of the cake in the tin to separate it from the side; this helps to prevent cracking. Cool completely, then refrigerate overnight.

◆ To serve, run a knife around the edge of the tin to loosen the cheesecake. Remove the side of the tin. If you like, slide the knife under the crust to separate the cheesecake from the base then, with a palette knife, slide on to a serving plate. Alternatively, leave the cheesecake on the tin base to avoid breaking the crust or surface and serve from the tin base.

◆ Dust the top of the cheesecake with cocoa or decorate with white and dark chocolate curls.

White Chocolate and Coconut Layer Cake

SERVES 12-16

*100 g (4 oz) good-quality white
chocolate, chopped*
120 ml (4 fl oz) whipping cream
120 ml (4 fl oz) milk
15 ml (1 tbsp) light rum
100 g (4 oz) unsalted butter, softened
175 g (6 oz) sugar
3 eggs
225 g (8 oz) plain flour
1 tsp baking powder
pinch of salt
*75 g (3 oz) shredded sweetened
coconut*

White chocolate mousse
*425 g (15 oz) good-quality white
chocolate, chopped*
1 litre (1¾ pt) whipping cream
120 ml (4 fl oz) light rum
fresh coconut strips for decoration

◆ Preheat the oven to 180°C (350°F, Gas Mark 4). Grease and flour 23 cm (9 inch) round, 5 cm (2 inch) deep cake tins.

◆ In the top of a double boiler over a low heat, melt the chocolate with the cream, stirring until smooth. Stir in the milk and rum; set aside to cool.

◆ With an electric mixer, beat the butter with the sugar until pale and thick, about 5 minutes. Add the eggs, 1 at a time, beating well after each addition. In another bowl, stir together the flour, baking powder and salt. Alternately add the flour mixture and melted white chocolate in batches, just until blended; stir in half the coconut. Pour the batter into the tins and spread evenly.

◆ Bake for 20-25 minutes, until a fine skewer inserted in the centres comes out clean. Cool on a wire rack for 10 minutes. Unmould the cakes on to the wire rack and cool completely.

◆ Meanwhile, prepare the mousse. In a saucepan over a low heat, melt the white chocolate and 350 ml (12 fl oz) cream, stirring frequently until smooth. Stir in the rum, then pour into a bowl. Refrigerate for 1-1½ hours, until completely cold and thickened.

◆ Whip the remaining cream until soft peaks form. Stir 1 spoonful of cream into the mousse mixture to lighten, then fold in about 250 ml (8 fl oz) whipped cream.

◆ With a serrated knife, slice the cake layers in half horizontally, making 4 layers. Place 1 layer on a plate and spread one-sixth of the mousse on top. Sprinkle with one-third of the remaining coconut. Place a second layer on top and spread with one-sixth of mousse. Sprinkle with another third of coconut. Place a third layer on top and spread with another one-sixth of mousse and the remaining coconut. Cover with the last cake layer and cover the top and sides with the remaining mousse.

◆ Spread the remaining whipped cream over the top and sides of the cake and garnish with fresh coconut strips.

SWEET SUCCESS

If fresh coconut is unavailable, use shredded sweetened coconut for garnish. Spread 40 g (1½ oz) coconut on baking sheet and bake at 180°C (350°F, Gas Mark 4) for 10-12 minutes, stirring twice, until golden. Press into the sides and sprinkle on the top of the cake.

For fresh coconut strips, use a swivel-bladed vegetable peeler to make paper-thin strips from fresh coconut pieces. Leave the brown skin on the pieces to create a pretty edge.

Family Chocolate Cake

SERVES 8-10

75 g (3 oz) plain chocolate
50 g (2 oz) clear honey
100 g (4 oz) butter or margarine
75 g (3 oz) sugar
2 eggs
150 g (5 oz) self-raising flour
25 g (1 oz) unsweetened cocoa powder
1½ level tsp baking powder
1.25 ml (¼ tsp) vanilla essence
150 ml (¼ pt) milk

Icing
50 g (2 oz) plain chocolate
45 ml (3 tbsp) water
25 g (1 oz) butter
200 g (7 oz) icing sugar, sieved

◆ Preheat the oven to 180°C (350°F, Gas Mark 4). Put the chocolate and honey into a small bowl over a pan of hot water. Stir until the chocolate has melted. Cool.

◆ Cream together the butter or margarine and sugar until light and fluffy.

◆ Beat in the chocolate mixture, then the eggs.

◆ Sieve together the flour, cocoa powder and baking powder.

◆ Stir in the flour mixture a little at a time, alternately with the vanilla essence and milk.

◆ Pour the mixture into a lined 19 cm (7½ inch) round cake tin.

◆ Bake in the oven for about 45 minutes.

◆ Turn on to a wire rack, leaving the lining paper on the cake to form a collar.

◆ When the cake is cool, make the icing. Put the chocolate and water into a small saucepan and melt over a gentle heat.

◆ Remove from the heat and stir in the butter. When the butter has melted, beat in the icing sugar.

◆ Spread the icing over the top of the cake and swirl with a palette knife. When the icing is firm, remove the lining paper from the cake.

Saucy Chocolate Cake

SERVES 8

100 g (4 oz) plain flour
90 g (3½ oz) sugar
5 tbsp cocoa powder
2 tsp baking powder
½ tsp salt
175 ml (6 fl oz) milk
25 g (1 oz) butter
5 ml (1 tsp) vanilla essence

Topping
150 g (5 oz) light brown sugar
50 g (2 oz) chopped pecans (optional)
400 ml (14 fl oz) boiling water
icing sugar for dusting

◆ Preheat the oven to 180°C (350°F, Gas Mark 4). Lightly butter a 20 x 20 x 5 cm (8 x 8 x 2 inch) baking dish.

◆ Combine the flour, sugar, 3 tbsp of cocoa powder, baking powder and salt. Stir in the milk, butter and vanilla essence just until blended. Spoon into the dish and spread evenly.

◆ In another bowl, combine the brown sugar, chopped nuts and remaining cocoa; gradually stir in the boiling water until the sugar dissolves. Gently pour over the batter in the baking dish.

◆ Bake for 25-30 minutes, until the top of the cake springs back when touched with a fingertip. Cool for 30-40 minutes on a wire rack. Dust with icing sugar and serve warm or chilled.

Chocolate Pecan Torte

SERVES 16

200 g (7 oz) plain chocolate, chopped
150 g (5 oz) pieces unsalted butter
4 eggs
100 g (4 oz) sugar
10 ml (2 tsp) vanilla essence
90 g (3½ oz) ground pecans
24 pecan halves

Chocolate honeyglaze

100 g (4 oz) plain chocolate, chopped
50 g (2 oz) pieces unsalted butter
2 tbsp honey

SWEET SUCCESS

This cake can be baked 2-3 days ahead, wrapped tightly and refrigerated or even frozen. Bring to room temperature before glazing.

◆ Preheat the oven to 180°C (350°F, Gas Mark 4). Grease a 20 cm (8 inch), 5 cm (2 inch) deep springform tin; line the bottom with greaseproof paper and grease the paper. Wrap the bottom of the tin in foil.

◆ In a saucepan over a low heat, melt the chocolate and butter, stirring until smooth. Remove from the heat.

◆ With an electric mixer, beat the eggs with sugar and vanilla essence just until frothy, 1-2 minutes. Stir in the melted chocolate and ground nuts until well blended. Pour into the tin and tap gently on a work surface to break any large air bubbles.

◆ Place the tin into a larger roasting tin and pour boiling water into the roasting tin, about 2 cm (¾ inch) up the side of the springform tin. Bake for 25-30 minutes, until the edge of the cake is set, but the centre is still soft. Remove the tin from the water-bath and remove the foil. Cool on a wire rack completely.

◆ Meanwhile, place the pecan halves on a baking sheet and bake for 10-12 minutes, until just brown, stirring occasionally.

◆ In a saucepan over a low heat, melt the chocolate, butter and honey, stirring until smooth; remove from the heat. Carefully dip the roasted nuts halfway into the glaze and place on a greaseproof paper-lined baking sheet until set. The glaze will have thickened slightly.

◆ Remove the side of the tin and turn the cake on to a wire rack placed over a baking sheet to catch any drips. Remove the tin bottom and paper so the bottom of cake is now the top. Pour the thickened glaze over the cake, tilting the rack slightly to spread the glaze. If necessary, use a palette knife to smooth the sides. Arrange the nuts around the outside edge of the torte and leave the glaze to set. With a palette knife, carefully slide the cake on to a serving dish.

Dobos Torte

SERVES 8

6 eggs, separated
zest of 1 lemon, grated
175 g (6 oz) sugar
150 g (5 oz) plain flour, sieved

Butter cream
225 g (8 oz) plain chocolate
225 g (8 oz) butter
450 g (1 lb) icing sugar, sieved

Caramel
175 g (6 oz) granulated sugar

◆ Preheat the oven to 200°C (400°F, Gas Mark 6). Grease and flour 7 flat surfaces, such as baking sheets and roasting tins. Using a cake tin or plate, mark a circle 20 cm (8 inch) in diameter on each one.

◆ Whisk the egg yolks with the lemon zest and sugar in a mixing bowl until the mixture is thick.

◆ Whisk the egg whites until stiff.

◆ Fold the egg whites and flour alternately into the egg yolk mixture.

◆ Divide the mixture evenly between the circles. Bake in batches in the oven for about 8 minutes, or until golden brown. Lift on to wire racks to cool.

◆ Use the 20 cm (8 inch) cake tin or plate to trim the edges so that all the circles are the same size.

◆ To make the butter cream, melt the chocolate. Add the butter and stir until melted. Cool. Beat in the sieved icing sugar.

◆ To make the caramel, put the sugar into a heavy saucepan. Heat very slowly over a low heat, stirring until the sugar is completely dissolved. Heat until the caramel turns golden brown.

◆ Pour the caramel immediately on to one of the cake layers. Before the caramel sets, cut the cake layer into 8 sections, using an oiled or buttered knife.

◆ Sandwich the remaining cake layers together with some of the chocolate butter cream. Spread butter cream round the sides of the cake.

◆ Put the remaining butter cream into a piping bag, fitted with a star nozzle. Pipe eight long whirls on top of the cake, radiating out from the centre. Set a caramel-coated section, tilted slightly, on each whirl.

Chocolate and Raspberry Torte

Serves 10

10 g (4 oz) plain chocolate, chopped
100 g (4 oz) ground blanched almonds
25 g (1 oz) plain flour
100 g (4 oz) butter, softened
100 g (4 oz) sugar
4 eggs, separated
¼ tsp cream of tartar

**Chocolate and raspberry ganache
icing and filling**
25 ml (8 fl oz) double cream
25 ml (8 fl oz) seedless raspberry jam
275 g (10 oz) plain chocolate, chopped
25 g (1 oz) butter, cut into pieces
60 ml (4 tbsp) raspberry-flavour
liqueur
225 g (8 oz) fresh raspberries, 8 or 10
reserved to decorate
chocolate leaves (see page 19) to
decorate

Variation

*For a lighter look, beat the icing
with a hand-held beater for 30-45
seconds until light and fluffy.
Immediately ice and decorate the
torte before the icing hardens.*

◆ Preheat the oven to 180°C (350°F, Gas Mark 4). Grease the bottom and sides of a 39 x 26 x 2.5 cm (15½ x 10½ x 1 inch) Swiss roll tin. Line the bottom with greaseproof paper, allowing 2.5 cm (1 inch) overhang; grease and flour the paper.

◆ In the top of a double boiler over a low heat, melt the chocolate, stirring frequently until smooth. Set aside to cool.

◆ In a bowl, mix the ground almonds and flour until blended. In another bowl, with an electric mixer, beat the butter and half the sugar until pale and creamy, about 3 minutes. Add the egg yolks, 1 at a time, beating well after each addition. Slowly beat in the melted chocolate until well blended, scraping the bowl occasionally.

◆ In a large bowl, with an electric mixer, beat the egg whites with the cream of tartar until stiff peaks form. Gradually sprinkle the remaining sugar over the egg whites in 2 batches, beating until the egg whites are stiff and glossy.

◆ Stir 1 spoonful of egg whites into the chocolate mixture to lighten, then fold in the remaining egg whites and the almond and flour mixture alternately just until blended. Spoon into the tin, spreading evenly.

◆ Bake for 10-12 minutes, or until the cake springs back when touched with a fingertip.

◆ Cool the cake in the tin on a wire rack for 10 minutes. Using the paper corners as a guide, lift the cake out of the tin on to the rack to cool completely.

◆ Meanwhile, prepare the icing. In a saucepan, bring the cream and half the raspberry jam to the boil. Remove from the heat and immediately stir in the chocolate until melted and smooth. Beat in the butter and half the raspberry-flavour liqueur. Cool the icing mixture, then refrigerate until it reaches a spreading consistency, about 1 hour; stir occasionally.

◆ Turn the cake on to a work surface, bottom side up. Trim the cake edges and cut the cake crosswise into 3 equal strips. In a saucepan, melt the remaining jam and raspberry-flavour liqueur, stirring until smooth; spoon equally over each cake strip and leave to soak in, 2-3 minutes.

◆ Place 1 cake strip on a wire rack over a baking sheet to catch the drips. Spread with about 250 ml (8 fl oz) chilled icing. Sprinkle with half the raspberries. Top with the second cake strip and spread with 250 ml (8 fl oz) icing and remaining raspberries. Place the third cake strip on top, top side up. With a palette knife, spread the remaining icing over the top and sides of the torte. Leave to set.

◆ With a palette knife, slide the torte on to a serving dish. Decorate the top of the torte with chocolate leaves and the reserved raspberries.

Sachertorte

SERVES 8

225 g (8 oz) plain chocolate
100 g (4 oz) unsalted butter
175 g (6 oz) caster sugar
5 eggs, separated
75 g (3 oz) ground hazelnuts
or almonds
50 g (2 oz) self-raising flour, sieved

Filling
150 ml (¼ pt) double cream, whipped

Icing
225 g (8 oz) plain chocolate
100 g (4 oz) butter, melted

To decorate
whipped cream
whole hazelnuts
chocolate leaves (see page 19)

◆ Preheat the oven to 180°C (350°F, Gas Mark 4). Melt the chocolate in a bowl over a saucepan of hot water. Add the butter, cut into small pieces, and beat until the butter has melted and the mixture is smooth.
◆ Beat in the caster sugar. Gradually add the egg yolks, beating well between each addition.
◆ Whisk the egg whites until stiff. Gently fold into the chocolate, with the ground nuts and flour.
◆ Put the mixture into two greased and base-lined 20 cm (8 inch) sandwich cake tins. Bake for 20-25 minutes. Cool on a wire rack.
◆ When the cakes are cold, sandwich together with whipped cream.
◆ To make the icing, melt the chocolate and gradually add the butter, beating well between each addition. Leave for 20-30 minutes, until cold, and of a coating consistency.

◆ Spread the icing over the top and sides of the cake. Leave until set.
◆ Decorate with piped whipped cream, hazelnuts and chocolate leaves.

Torta Sorentina (Easter Cake)

SERVES 8

225 g (8 oz) unsalted butter
4 large eggs
225 g (8 oz) sugar
225 g (8 oz) self-raising flour
zest of ½ lemon, grated

Lemon filling
1 egg white
50 g (2 oz) icing sugar
75 g (3 oz) unsalted butter
zest of ½ lemon, grated

Icing
175 g (6 oz) plain chocolate
2 tbsp cream
25 g (1 oz) butter
crystallized lemon slices, to decorate

◆ Preheat the oven to 180°C (350°F, Gas Mark 4). Melt the butter and leave to cool.
◆ Put the eggs and sugar into a bowl over a pan of hot water and whisk until they are pale and thick and the whisk leaves a trail.
◆ Gently fold in the flour, lemon zest and butter. Do not overmix.
◆ Pour into a greased and floured 2 litre (3½ pt) ring mould. Bake in the oven for 30-40 minutes. Cool slightly, then turn out on to a wire rack.
◆ To make the filling, put the egg white and icing sugar into a bowl over a pan of hot water and whisk until a meringue is formed. Remove from the heat and whisk until cool.
◆ Beat the butter until light and fluffy. Beat in the meringue a little at a time. Add the lemon zest.
◆ Split the cake into 3 layers. Spread the lemon filling between the layers. Chill.

◆ Put the chocolate and cream in a bowl over a pan of hot water. When melted, stir in the butter. Remove from heat and mix until smooth.
◆ Coat the cake with the icing. Decorate with crystallized lemon slices. Allow icing to set before serving.

Easy Chocolate Truffle Cake

SERVES 16-20

250 g (9 oz) plain chocolate, chopped
225 g (8 oz) pieces unsalted butter
75 g (3 oz) sugar
120 ml (4 fl oz) whipping cream
15 ml (1 tbsp) vanilla essence
6 eggs

Chocolate glaze
175 g (6 oz) plain chocolate, chopped
50 g (2 oz) butter, cut into pieces

To decorate
whipped cream
rose petals

◆ Preheat the oven to 180°C (350°F, Gas Mark 4). Grease a 23 cm (9 inch), 5 cm (2 inch) deep round springform tin; line the bottom with greaseproof paper and grease the paper. Wrap the bottom of the tin in foil.
◆ Melt the chocolate, butter and sugar with the cream, stirring until smooth; cool slightly. Stir in the vanilla essence.
◆ Beat the eggs lightly, about 1 minute. Slowly beat the chocolate into the eggs until blended.
◆ Place the tin into larger roasting tin and pour boiling water into the roasting tin, about 2 cm (¾ inch) up the sides of the springform tin. Bake for 25-30 minutes, until the edge of the cake is set, but the centre is still soft. Remove the tin from water-bath and remove the foil. Cool on a wire rack completely; the cake will sink in the centre and may be cracked.

◆ Remove the side of the tin and turn the cake on to a wire rack placed over a baking sheet to catch any drips. Remove the base and paper.
◆ In a saucepan over a low heat, melt the chocolate and butter, stirring until smooth. Pour over the cake, tilting the rack slightly to spread the glaze.
◆ With a palette knife, carefully slide the cake on to a serving dish. If you like, pipe a whipped cream border around the edge. Dip the rose petals in lightly beaten egg white, then in caster sugar. Allow to stand on greaseproof paper in a cool place for about 2 hours. Place in the centre of the cake. Serve with softly whipped cream on the side.

RIGHT *Easy Chocolate Truffle Cake*

Blackout Cake

SERVES 12-16

300 g (11 oz) plain flour
25 g (1 oz) cocoa powder
1 tbsp bicarbonate of soda
½ tsp salt
100 g (4 oz) plain chocolate, chopped
175 g (6 oz) unsalted butter, softened
350 g (12 oz) sugar
3 eggs
10 ml (2 tsp) vanilla essence
175 ml (6 fl oz) buttermilk
or 1 tbsp instant coffee in
350 ml (12 fl oz) boiling water

Chocolate ganache icing
300 ml (10 fl oz) double cream
450 g (1 lb) plain chocolate, chopped
50 g (2 oz) butter, cut into pieces
10 ml (2 tsp) vanilla essence
grated chocolate to decorate
icing sugar for dusting

◆ Preheat the oven to 180°C (350°F, Gas Mark 4). Grease and flour 23 cm (9 inch) round, 5 cm (2 inch) deep cake tins.
◆ Stir together the flour, cocoa powder and bicarbonate of soda and salt. In the top of a double boiler over a low heat, melt the chocolate; set aside.
◆ In a second bowl with an electric mixer, beat the butter with the sugar until light and creamy, about 5 minutes. Add the eggs, 1 at a time, beating well after each addition. Beat in the chocolate and vanilla essence.
◆ Add the flour mixture to the batter in 2 additions alternately with the buttermilk; beat just until blended. At low speed, slowly beat in the boiling coffee until smooth, scraping the bowl once; the batter will be thin. Pour into the prepared tins.

◆ Bake for 25-30 minutes, or until a fine skewer inserted in the centres comes out with just a few crumbs attached. Cool in the tins on a wire rack for 10 minutes. Unmould and cool completely.
◆ Meanwhile, prepare the icing. In a medium saucepan bring the cream to the boil. Remove from the heat and immediately stir in the chocolate until melted and smooth. Beat in the butter and vanilla. Cool; refrigerate for 45-55 minutes or until the icing is soft but spreadable.
◆ Place 1 cake layer on a plate and cover with one-third of the icing. Place the second layer on top and ice the top and sides with the remaining icing. Press the grated chocolate on to the sides of the cake and sprinkle on top. Dust the top with icing sugar.

Mushroom Cake

SERVES 6

25 g (1 oz) unsweetened cocoa powder
15 ml (1 tbsp) boiling water
100 g (4 oz) butter or margarine
100 g (4 oz) light, soft brown sugar
2 eggs, beaten
100 g (4 oz) self-raising flour

Icing
100 g (4 oz) butter or margarine
225 g (8 oz) icing sugar
50 g (2 oz) plain chocolate, melted
225 g (8 oz) marzipan (preferably
"white")
apricot jam, sieved
icing sugar or drinking chocolate

◆ Preheat the oven to 180°C (350°F, Gas Mark 4). Mix together the cocoa powder and water to form a paste.
◆ Put the butter or margarine, sugar and chocolate paste into a bowl and beat until light and fluffy.
◆ Beat in the eggs a little at a time.
◆ Fold in the flour.
◆ Spread the mixture into 1 greased and base-lined, 20 cm (8 inch) sandwich cake tin. Bake in the oven for about 25 minutes. Turn out and cool.
◆ To make the icing, cream together the butter or margarine and icing sugar. Stir in the melted chocolate and beat well. Cool.
◆ Using a piping bag fitted with a star nozzle, pipe lines of icing from the edge of the cake to the centre, to

represent the underside of a mushroom.
◆ Reserve a small piece of marzipan for the stalk. Roll the remaining marzipan out to a strip about 60 cm (24 inch) long and wide enough to stand just above the sides of the cake.
◆ Brush the sides of the cake with apricot jam. Press the marzipan strip round the edge of the cake. Curve the top of the marzipan over the piped ridges.
◆ Shape the reserved marzipan into a stalk and place in the centre of the cake. Sieve a little icing sugar or drinking chocolate over the icing on the cake.

Surprise Chocolate Ring

SERVES 8

150 g (5 oz) self-raising flour
25 g (1 oz) unsweetened cocoa powder
175 g (6 oz) soft margarine
175 g (6 oz) sugar
3 eggs
60 ml (4 tbsp) cherry brandy
100 g (4 oz) fruit (eg strawberries,
raspberries, stoned cherries)
150 ml (¼ pt) double cream

Icing
65 ml (2½ fl oz) double cream
175 g (6 oz) plain chocolate, grated

To decorate
Piped chocolate butterflies
(see page 19) or
chocolate dipped fruits

◆ Preheat the oven to 180°C (350°F, Gas Mark 4). Sieve the flour and cocoa into a mixing bowl. Add the margarine, sugar and eggs. Beat well together.

◆ Spoon the mixture into a greased and floured 1.2 litre (2 pt) ring mould. Bake in the oven for about 35-40 minutes. Turn out and cool.

◆ Turn the cake upside down and cut a slice about 2 cm (¾ inch) deep off the flat base of the ring. Lift off the slice carefully and reserve.

◆ With a teaspoon, scoop out the cake in a channel about 2 cm (¾ inch) deep and 2.5 cm (1 inch) wide.

◆ Sprinkle 45 ml (3 tbsp) of the cherry brandy over the sponge.

◆ Chop the fruit and spread in the hollow.

◆ Whisk the cream until stiff. Stir in the remaining brandy. Spread the cream over the fruit.

◆ Place the reserved slice back on the cake.

◆ Invert the cake so it is the right way up.

◆ To make the icing, put the cream into a saucepan and bring just to the boil. Add the chocolate. Stir until the chocolate melts.

◆ Cool until the mixture is thick and smooth. Pour over the cake.

◆ Put in a cool place until set.

◆ Decorate with piped chocolate butterflies or chocolate dipped fruit.

Chocolate Meringue Gâteau

SERVES 6

3 egg whites
pinch of cream of tartar
150 g (5 oz) caster sugar
75 g (3 oz) ground hazelnuts

Sponge
50 g (2 oz) plain flour
50 g (2 oz) unsweetened cocoa powder
4 eggs, separated
100 g (4 oz) sugar

Chocolate cream
225 g (8 oz) plain chocolate
2 egg yolks
30 ml (2 tbsp) water
300 ml (½ pt) double cream
50 g (2 oz) sugar
red jam

To decorate
mixed chopped nuts
chocolate curls
icing sugar

◆ Preheat the oven to 150°C (300°F, Gas Mark 2). Line 2 baking sheets with greaseproof paper. Draw an 18 cm (7 inch) circle on each one.

◆ Put the egg whites and cream of tartar into a bowl and whisk until stiff.

◆ Whisk in the sugar a little at a time until the mixture is thick and glossy. Fold in the nuts.

◆ Spread or pipe the meringue in the circles marked on the paper. Bake in the oven for 1 hour. Turn off the heat and leave to dry in the closed oven for a further 30 minutes, or until crisp.

◆ Remove and cool. Carefully peel away the paper.

◆ Preheat the oven to 180°C (350°F, Gas Mark 4). To make the sponge, sieve together the flour and cocoa.

◆ Whisk together the egg yolks and sugar until the mixture is thick and pale.

◆ Whisk the egg whites until thick, but not stiff.

◆ Fold the flour and egg whites alternately into the egg yolk mixture.

◆ Pour into a greased and lined 18 cm (7 inch) cake tin. Bake for about 40 minutes. Remove and cool.

◆ To make the chocolate cream, melt the chocolate. Cool slightly. Beat together the egg yolks and water.

◆ Stir the melted chocolate into the egg yolks, mixing well. Put in a pan and cook very gently for a minute. Cool.

◆ Beat together the cream and sugar until soft peaks form. Fold into the chocolate mixture. Cover and chill.

◆ To assemble the gâteau, cut the cake into 2 layers and spread each with a little red jam.

◆ Put a meringue round on a plate and spread with a little chocolate cream. Top with a layer of sponge, spread with cream and place the second meringue round on top. Spread with cream and place the second layer of sponge on top.

◆ Spread remaining chocolate cream on the top and sides of the cake.

◆ Put chopped nuts round the side of the cake. Top with chocolate curls and sprinkle with icing sugar.

Black Forest Gâteau

SERVES 10

65 g (2½ oz) light plain flour
40 g (1½ oz) cocoa powder
½ tsp baking powder
5 eggs, separated
200 g (7 oz) sugar
¼ tsp cream of tartar
65 g (2½ oz) butter, melted and cooled

Cherry filling
425 g (15 oz) black cherries in juice or
syrup, stoned
75 ml (5 tbsp) cherry-flavour liqueur
2 tbsp cornflour, dissolved in
30 ml (2 tbsp) water
475 ml (16 fl oz) whipping cream
2 tbsp caster sugar

To decorate
Chocolate curls (see page 18)
glacé or maraschino cherries

◆ Preheat the oven to 180°C (350°F, Gas Mark 4). Grease the bottom and sides of a 20 cm (8 inch) springform tin. Line the bottom with greaseproof paper; grease the paper and flour the tin.

◆ Sift together the flour, cocoa powder and baking powder. Beat the egg yolks with 175 g (6 oz) sugar until pale and thick, about 5 minutes.
◆ Beat the egg whites and cream of tartar until stiff peaks form. Sprinkle in the remaining sugar and beat until stiff and glossy.
◆ Stir 1 spoonful of egg whites into the yolk mixture to lighten. Fold in the flour and cocoa mixture and the remaining egg whites alternately just until blended. Pour the melted butter over and fold in just until blended. Spoon into the tin, spreading evenly.
◆ Bake for 30-35 minutes, until a fine skewer inserted in the centre comes out clean. Cool on a wire rack for 10 minutes. Remove the tin and cool completely.
◆ Meanwhile, prepare the filling. Drain the cherries, reserving the juice. Mix 3 tbsp cherry juice with 3 tbsp cherry-flavour liqueur; set aside. In a saucepan, stir together the remaining cherry juice and cornflour mixture. Bring to the boil, then simmer for 2-3 minutes, until thickened. Stir in the cherries and set aside to cool.

◆ Whip the cream, sugar and remaining cherry-flavour liqueur until soft peaks form. Reserve about 120 ml (4 fl oz) cream for decoration.
◆ With a serrated knife, cut the cake horizontally into 3 layers. Place the bottom layer on a plate. Sprinkle over one-third of the cherry juice syrup and spread with about 350 ml (12 fl oz) whipped cream. Spoon half the cherry mixture evenly over the cream and cover with a second cake layer. Sprinkle one-third of the cherry juice syrup over and another 350 ml (12 fl oz) whipped cream. Spoon the remaining cherry mixture over. Sprinkle the cut side of the third cake layer with the remaining cherry juice syrup and place cut side down over the cherry layer. Ice the top and sides of the cake with the remaining whipped cream.
◆ Press chocolate curls on to the sides of the cake. Spoon the reserved cream into a small piping bag fitted with a medium star nozzle and pipe 10 rosettes evenly around the cake. Top each with a glacé or maraschino cherry. Refrigerate.

Classic Devil's Food Cake

SERVES 10-12

50 g (2 oz) plain chocolate, chopped
65 g (2½ oz) cocoa powder
250 g (9 oz) plain flour
2 tsp bicarbonate of soda
½ tsp salt
150 g (5 oz) unsalted butter, softened
425 g (15 oz) soft brown sugar
15 ml (1 tbsp) vanilla essence
3 eggs
175 ml (6 fl oz) soured cream
5 ml (1 tsp) vinegar
250 ml (8 fl oz) boiling water

Chocolate ganache icing
675 ml (24 fl oz) whipping cream
675 g (1½ lb) plain chocolate, chopped
15 ml (1 tbsp) vanilla essence

RIGHT *Classic Devil's Food Cake*

◆ Preheat the oven to 190°C (375°F, Gas Mark 5). Butter 2 23 cm (9 inch) round cake tins, 4 cm (1½ inch) deep. Line the bottoms with greaseproof paper; butter the paper and flour the tins.

◆ In the top of a double boiler over a low heat, melt the chocolate, stirring frequently until smooth. Set aside. Sift together the cocoa powder, flour, bicarbonate of soda and salt.

◆ With an electric mixer, cream the butter, brown sugar and vanilla essence until light and creamy, about 5 minutes, scraping the side of the bowl occasionally. Add the eggs, 1 at a time, beating well after each addition.

◆ Add the flour mixture alternately with the soured cream in 3 batches, beating until well blended. Stir in the vinegar and slowly beat in the boiling water; the batter will be thin. Pour into the tins.

◆ Bake for 20-25 minutes, until a fine skewer inserted in the centre comes out with just a few crumbs attached.

Cool the cakes in tins on a wire rack. Remove the cakes from the tins. Remove from the paper and cool on a wire rack while preparing the icing.

◆ In a saucepan over a medium heat, bring the cream to the boil. Remove from the heat and stir in the chocolate all at once until melted and smooth. Cool slightly. Pour into a large bowl and refrigerate for 1 hour, stirring twice, until the icing is spreadable.

◆ With a serrated knife, slice each cake layer horizontally into 2 layers. Place 1 cake layer cut-side up on a cake plate and spread with one-sixth of the icing. Place a second layer on top and cover with another sixth of the icing. Place a third layer on top and cover with another sixth of the icing, then cover with the fourth cake layer top-side (rounded) up. Ice the top and sides of the cake with the remaining sugar. Serve at room temperature.

Refrigerator Biscuit Cake

SERVES 6

225 g (8 oz) milk chocolate
100 g (4 oz) butter
50 g (2 oz) golden syrup
50 g (2 oz) raisins, soaked overnight in a little rum
50 g (2 oz) Brazil nuts, roughly chopped
50 g (2 oz) glacé cherries, roughly chopped
225 g (8 oz) digestive biscuits, crushed

To decorate
glacé cherries
whole Brazil nuts

◆ Put the chocolate, butter and golden syrup into a bowl over a pan of hot water.

◆ When the chocolate has melted, stir in the raisins, nuts and cherries.

◆ Add the biscuits and mix well together.

◆ Line a 450 g (1 lb) loaf tin with greaseproof paper. Press the mixture into the tin.

◆ Chill for at least 4 hours, preferably overnight.

◆ Turn out and decorate with glacé cherries and Brazil nuts.

Chocolate-Chestnut Roulade

SERVES 12

Roulade sponge
175 g (6 oz) plain chocolate, chopped
120 ml (4 fl oz) strong coffee
6 eggs, separated
6 tbsp caster sugar
½ tsp cream of tartar
10 ml (2 tsp) vanilla essence
cocoa powder for dusting

Chestnut cream filling
450 ml (16 fl oz) double cream
30 ml (2 tbsp) coffee-flavour liqueur
or 10 ml (2 tsp) vanilla essence
475 ml (16 fl oz) canned sweetened
chestnut purée

To decorate
icing sugar
chopped marrons

◆ Preheat the oven to 180°C (350°F, Gas Mark 4). Grease the base and sides of a 39 x 26 x 2.5 cm (15½ x 10½ x 1 inch) Swiss roll tin. Line the base with greaseproof paper, allowing 2.5 cm (1 inch) to overhang; grease and flour the paper.

◆ Melt the chocolate with the coffee, stirring frequently until smooth. Set aside.

◆ Beat the egg yolks with half the sugar until pale and thick, about 5 minutes. Slowly beat in the chocolate just until blended.

◆ In another large bowl, with an electric mixer, beat the egg whites and cream of tartar until stiff peaks form. Gradually sprinkle the sugar over the egg whites in 2 batches and continue beating until the egg whites are stiff and glossy; beat in the vanilla essence.

◆ Stir 1 spoonful of egg whites into the chocolate mixture to lighten, then fold in the remaining egg whites. Spoon into the prepared tin, spreading evenly.

◆ Bake for 12-15 minutes, or until the cake springs back when touched with a fingertip.

◆ Meanwhile, dust a tea towel with cocoa powder. When the cake is done, turn out on to the towel immediately and remove the paper. Starting at a narrow end, roll the cake and towel together Swiss-roll fashion. Cool completely.

◆ With an electric mixer, whip the cream and coffee-flavour liqueur or vanilla essence until soft peaks form. Beat 1 spoonful of cream into the chestnut purée to lighten, then fold in the remaining cream.

◆ Unroll the cake and trim the edges. Spread the chestnut cream mixture to within 2.5 cm (1 inch) of the edge of the cake. Using the towel to lift the cake, roll the cake.

◆ Place the roulade seam-side down on a serving plate. Decorate the roulade with bands of sifted icing sugar and chopped marrons.

Buche de Noël

SERVES 6-8

4 eggs, separated
100 g (4 oz) sugar
100 g (4 oz) plain flour

Butter cream
75 g (3 oz) sugar
85 ml (3 fl oz) water
4 egg yolks
175 g (6 oz) unsalted butter
75 g (3 oz) plain chocolate, melted
5-10 ml (1-2 tsp) dark rum

To decorate
Meringue Mushrooms (see page 134)
marzipan, holly leaves and berries

◆ Preheat the oven to 230°C (450°F, Gas Mark 8). Grease and line a 23 x 33 cm (9 x 13 inch) Swiss roll tin.

◆ Put the egg yolks and sugar into a mixing bowl and whisk until the mixture falls in a thick trail.
◆ Whisk the egg whites until stiff.
◆ Fold the egg whites and flour alternately into the egg yolk mixture. Pour into the tin and bake in the oven for about 10 minutes until golden brown.
◆ Put a sheet of greaseproof paper on top of a dampened tea towel and sprinkle with caster sugar. Turn the sponge out on to the sugared paper.
◆ Peel off the lining paper and quickly trim the edges of the sponge. Make a shallow groove across one short side of the cake 2.5 cm (1 inch) from the edge.
◆ Fold the sponge over at the groove. Using the towel as support, roll up the sponge with the greaseproof paper inside. Cover with the damp cloth until cold.
◆ To make the butter cream, put the sugar and water into a small pan. Dissolve the sugar and then bring to

the boil and boil to the "thread" stage (110°C/225°F).
◆ Whisk the egg yolks in a bowl until thick and creamy. Slowly pour the hot syrup on to the egg yolks in a steady stream, beating constantly until the mixture is light and fluffy.
◆ Beat the butter until soft. Add the egg mixture a little at a time until the mixture is firm and shiny. Stir in the chocolate and rum.
◆ Carefully unroll the sponge and remove the greaseproof paper. Spread a little butter cream over the sponge and roll up again.
◆ Put the cake on to a serving dish. Spoon the remaining butter cream into a piping bag fitted with a star nozzle. Pipe lines lengthways down the cake. Add an occasional swirl to represent a "knot" on a log.
◆ Decorate with Meringue Mushrooms and marzipan, holly leaves and berries.

Pies and Pastries

Chocolate Chiffon Pie   69

Chocolate and Pecan Pie   70

Chocolate Cream Pie   71

White Chocolate Mousse and Strawberry Tart   72

Rich Chocolate Meringue Pie   74

Mississippi Mud Pie   75

Black-Bottom Lemon Tartlets   76

Mocha-Fudge Pie with Espresso Custard Cream   78

White Chocolate and Banana Cream Tart   79

Chocolate and Pine Nut Tart   80

Chocolate Syrup Tart   82

Chocolate Truffle Tart   83

Chocolate Chiffon Pie

SERVES 6-8

175 g (6 oz) shortcrust pastry
150 ml (¼ pt) milk
75 g (3 oz) sugar
100 g (4 oz) plain chocolate, chopped
2 small eggs, separated
2 tsp powdered gelatine
30 ml (2 tbsp) water
150 ml (¼ pt) double cream

To decorate
whipped cream
chocolate curls (see page 18)

◆ Preheat the oven to 190°C (375°F, Gas Mark 5). Roll out the pastry and use to line a 20 cm (8 inch) flan tin. Bake "blind" (lined with greaseproof paper and baking beans) in the oven for 20-25 minutes. Remove the greaseproof paper and baking beans and return to the oven for a further 5-10 minutes until crisp and lightly browned. Leave to cool.

◆ Put the milk, 25 g (½ oz) sugar and chocolate into a saucepan and melt over a gentle heat. Stir continuously. Cool slightly.

◆ Whisk the egg yolks into the chocolate mixture.

◆ Dissolve the gelatine in the water and stir into the chocolate. Leave until the mixture is beginning to thicken and set.

◆ Whisk the egg whites until stiff. Whisk in the remaining sugar.

◆ Whisk the cream until it stands in soft peaks.

◆ Fold the egg whites and cream thoroughly into the chocolate mixture. Pour into the pastry case. Chill until set.

◆ To serve, pipe whipped cream over the top and pile chocolate curls in the centre.

Chocolate and Pecan Pie

SERVES 8-10

150 g (5 oz) plain flour
1 tbsp caster sugar
½ tsp salt
100 g (4 oz) small pieces butter
120 ml (4 fl oz) iced water

Filling

75 g (3 oz) plain chocolate, chopped
25 g (1 oz) butter, cut into pieces
3 eggs
50 g (2 oz) light brown sugar
75 ml (3 fl oz) golden syrup
15 ml (1 tbsp) vanilla essence
175 g (6 oz) pecan halves
75 g (3 oz) milk or plain chocolate
chips (optional)

◆ Prepare the piecrust. In a food processor fitted with a metal blade, process the flour, sugar and salt to blend. Add the butter and process for 15-20 seconds, until the mixture resembles coarse crumbs. With the machine running, add iced water through the feeder tube, just until the dough begins to stick together; do not allow the dough to form a ball or the pastry will be tough.

◆ Turn the dough on to a floured work surface, shape into a flat disc and wrap tightly in clingfilm. Refrigerate for 1 hour.

◆ Lightly butter a 23 cm (9 inch) pie dish, 4 cm (1½ inch) deep. Soften the dough for 10-15 minutes at room temperature. On a well-floured surface, roll out the dough into a 30 cm (12 inch) circle about 5mm (¼ inch) thick. Roll the dough loosely around the rolling pin and unroll over the pie dish; ease the dough into the dish.

◆ With kitchen scissors, trim the dough, leaving about a 5 mm (¼ inch) overhang; flatten to the rim of the pie dish, pressing slightly towards the centre of the dish. With a small knife, cut out hearts or other shapes from the dough trimmings. Brush the dough edge with water and press the dough shapes to the edge. Prick the bottom of dough with a fork. Refrigerate for 30 minutes.

◆ Preheat the oven to 200°C (400°F, Gas Mark 6). Line the pie shell with foil or greaseproof paper and fill with dry beans or rice. Bake for 5 minutes, then lift out foil or paper with the beans and bake for 5 minutes longer.

Remove to a wire rack to cool slightly. Lower the oven temperature to 190°C (375°F, Gas Mark 5).

◆ In a saucepan over a low heat, melt the chocolate and butter, stirring until smooth. Set aside.

◆ In a bowl, beat together the eggs, sugar, golden syrup and vanilla essence. Slowly beat in the melted chocolate. Sprinkle the pecan halves and chocolate chips (if using) over the bottom of the pastry. Place the pie dish on a baking sheet and carefully pour in the chocolate mixture.

◆ Bake for 35-40 minutes, until the chocolate mixture is set; the top may crack slightly. If the pastry edges begin to overbrown, cover with strips of foil. Transfer to a wire rack to cool. Serve warm with softly whipped cream.

Chocolate Cream Pie

SERVES 8

225 g (8 oz) plain chocolate digestive
biscuits
50 g (2 oz) butter, melted
175 g (6 oz) plain chocolate, chopped
250 ml (8 fl oz) whipping cream
40 g (1½ oz) cornflour
1 tbsp plain flour
50 g (2 oz) caster sugar
675 ml (22 fl oz) milk
5 egg yolks
40 g (1½ oz) butter, softened

Light whipped cream
350 ml (12 fl oz) double cream
2 egg whites
¼ tsp cream of tartar
50 g (2 oz) sugar
10 ml (2 tsp) vanilla essence
cocoa powder for dusting

◆ Preheat the oven to 180°C (350°F,
Gas Mark 4). Lightly butter a 23 cm
(9 inch), 4 cm (1½ inch) deep pie dish
or fluted baking dish.
◆ In a food processor, process the
chocolate biscuits until fine crumbs
form. Pour in the melted butter and
process just until blended. Pat on to
the bottom and sides of the pie dish.

◆ Bake for 5-7 minutes, just until set.
Transfer to a wire rack to cool
completely.
◆ In a saucepan over low heat, melt
the chocolate with the whipping
cream, stirring until smooth. Set
aside.
◆ In another saucepan, combine the
cornflour, flour and sugar. Gradually
stir in the milk and cook over
medium heat until thickened and
bubbling.
◆ In a bowl, beat the egg yolks
lightly. Slowly pour 250 ml (8 fl oz)
hot milk into the yolks, stirring
constantly. Return the egg-yolk
mixture to the pan and bring to a
gentle boil, stirring constantly. Cook
for 1 minute longer. Stir in the butter
and melted chocolate until well
blended. Pour into the prepared crust
and place a piece of clingfilm directly
against the surface of the filling to
prevent a skin forming. Cool, then
refrigerate until completely chilled.
◆ With an electric mixer, whip the
cream until soft peaks form. In
another bowl, with an electric mixer
and clean blades, beat the egg whites
and cream of tartar until stiff peaks
form. Gradually sprinkle the sugar

over in 2 batches, beating well after
each addition, until the whites are
stiff and glossy. Beat in the vanilla
essence.
◆ Fold 1 spoonful of egg white into
the cream to lighten, then fold the
remaining egg whites into the cream.
Peel the clingfilm from the chilled
custard; spread the cream on to the
custard in a swirling pattern. Dust the
cream lightly with cocoa powder.

White Chocolate Mousse and Strawberry Tart

SERVES 10-12

100 g (4 oz) butter, softened
50 g (2 oz) caster sugar
½ tsp salt
3 egg yolks
5 ml (1 tsp) vanilla essence
150 g (5 oz) plain flour

Strawberry filling
900 g (2 lb) fresh, ripe strawberries
30 ml (2 tbsp) cherry-flavour liqueur

White chocolate mousse filling
250 g (9 oz) white chocolate, chopped
45 ml (3 tbsp) cherry-flavour liqueur
30 ml (2 tbsp) water
350 ml (12 fl oz) double cream
2 egg whites (optional)
1.5 ml (¼ tsp) cream of tartar
(optional)

To decorate
25 g (1 oz) white chocolate, melted, or
white chocolate curls (see page 18)
2 tbsp seedless strawberry jam, melted
and cooled

SWEET SUCCESS

Be sure to allow the melted white chocolate to cool to below body temperature so it does not deflate the whipped cream. A small dab should feel cool when touched to your upper lip, about 30°C (85°F). The tart shell can be made ahead, but the shell should be filled and assembled the same day it is to be served to prevent the berries from bleeding into the mousse mixture and the mousse from becoming too firm when refrigerated.

◆ Prepare the pastry. In a bowl, with a hand-held electric mixer, beat the butter with the sugar and salt until creamy, about 2 minutes. Add the egg yolks and vanilla essence and beat until smooth. Add half the flour to the butter and egg mixture, then stir in the remaining flour by hand until well blended.

◆ Place a piece of clingfilm on a work surface. Scrape the dough on to the clingfilm. Use the clingfilm to help shape the dough into a flat disc and wrap tightly. Refrigerate for 1 hour.

◆ Lightly butter a 25 cm (10 inch) tart tin with a removable base. Soften the dough for 10 minutes at room temperature. On a well-floured surface, roll out the dough to a 28-30 cm (11½-12 inch) circle about 3 mm (⅛ inch) thick. Roll the dough loosely around the rolling pin and unroll over the tart tin. Ease the dough into the tin, patching if necessary.

◆ With floured fingers, press the overhang down slightly toward the centre, making the top edge thicker. Roll the rolling pin over the tin edge to cut off the excess dough. Press the thicker top edge against the side of the tin to form a rim about 5 mm (¼ inch) higher than the tin. Using your thumb and forefinger, crimp the edge. Prick the bottom of the dough with a fork. Refrigerate for 1 hour.

◆ Preheat the oven to 190°C (375°F, Gas Mark 5). Line the tart shell with foil or greaseproof paper; fill with dry beans or rice. Bake for 10 minutes; lift out the foil or paper with the beans and bake for 5-7 minutes longer until set and golden. Remove to a wire rack to cool completely.

◆ Prepare the strawberry filling. Cut the strawberries in half lengthwise. In a bowl, mash about 350 g (12 oz) strawberry halves with the cherry-flavour liqueur. Set the remaining berries and the mashed berries aside.

◆ Prepare the mousse. In a saucepan over a low heat, melt the white chocolate with the cherry-flavour liqueur, water and 120 ml (4 fl oz) cream, stirring until smooth. Set aside to cool.

◆ With an electric mixer, beat the remaining cream until soft peaks form. Stir 1 spoonful of cream into the chocolate mixture to lighten, then fold in the remaining cream. If you like, beat the egg whites with the cream of tartar until stiff peaks form then fold them into the chocolate cream mixture to make a lighter, softer mousse.

◆ Pour about one-third of the mousse mixture into the cooled tart shell. Spread the mashed berries evenly over the mousse, then cover with the remaining mousse mixture.

◆ To serve, arrange the sliced strawberries cut side up in concentric circles around the tart to cover the mousse. Remove the side of the tin and slide the tart onto a serving plate. Spoon the melted white chocolate into a paper cone and drizzle the white chocolate over the tart; alternatively, decorate the centre with white chocolate curls, or glaze with seedless strawberry jam.

Rich Chocolate Meringue Pie

SERVES 6

225 g (8 oz) digestive biscuits
100 g (4 oz) butter

Filling
25 g (1 oz) sugar
25 g (1 oz) plain flour
2 level tsp cornflour
2 egg yolks
300 ml (½ pt) milk
25 g (1 oz) butter
100 g (4 oz) plain chocolate, finely
chopped
10 ml (2 tsp) rum (optional)

Topping
2 egg whites
100 g (4 oz) caster sugar
ground cinnamon

◆ Preheat the oven to 200°C (400°F, Gas Mark 6). Crush the biscuits until they resemble fine breadcrumbs.
◆ Melt the butter and stir into the biscuits. Press the biscuits over the base and sides of a 20 cm (8 inch) ovenproof flan dish.
◆ Blend together the sugar, flour, cornflour, egg yolks and a little of the milk. Heat the remaining milk.
◆ Stir the hot milk on to the flour mixture and whisk well. Return the mixture to the pan. Heat gently, stirring until the mixture thickens.
◆ Stir in the butter, chocolate and rum if used. Stir until smooth. Pour into the biscuit pie shell. Chill.
◆ About 30 minutes before serving, make the meringue topping. Whisk the egg whites until stiff.

◆ Whisk in half the sugar a teaspoonful at a time. Add the remaining sugar and whisk well.
◆ Spread the meringue over the chocolate flan. Swirl decoratively with a teaspoon.
◆ Bake in the oven for 3-5 minutes, until the meringue is golden brown.
◆ Sprinkle with a little ground cinnamon.

Mississippi Mud Pie

SERVES 8

175 g (6 oz) digestive biscuits
large knob of butter, melted
100 g (4 oz) plain chocolate, melted
1.2 litres (2 pt) coffee ice cream
1.2 litres (2 pt) chocolate ice cream
30 ml (2 tbsp) Tia Maria
30 ml (2 tbsp) brandy

To decorate
whipped cream
grated chocolate

◆ Crush the biscuits in a food processor or in a polythene bag with a rolling pin.
◆ Stir in the butter and chocolate and mix well together.
◆ Press the crumbs firmly and evenly over the bottom and sides of a greased 23 cm (9 inch) flan dish. Chill.
◆ Allow the ice creams to soften slightly. Put in a bowl and add the Tia Maria and brandy. Blend well together.
◆ Spoon the ice cream into the chocolate case and put in the freezer until solid.
◆ Remove the pie from the freezer about 15 minutes before serving. Decorate with whipped cream and grated chocolate.

Black-Bottom Lemon Tartlets

MAKES 12

175 g (6 oz) plain flour
2 tbsp icing sugar
½ tsp salt
175 g (6 oz) unsalted butter, cut into
pieces and at room temperature
1 egg yolk
2.5 ml (½ tsp) vanilla essence
30–45 ml (2-3 tbsp) cold water

Lemon custard sauce
1 lemon
350 ml (12 fl oz) milk
6 egg yolks
75 g (3 oz) sugar

Lemon curd filling
2 lemons
175 g (6 oz) unsalted butter,
cut into pieces
225 g (8 oz) sugar
3 eggs

Chocolate filling
175 ml (6 fl oz) cream
175 g (6 oz) plain chocolate, chopped
25 g (1 oz) unsalted butter,
cut into pieces

To decorate
Chocolate triangles (see page 18)
25 g (1 oz) plain chocolate, melted

SWEET SUCCESS

Pastry and tartlets can be prepared
a day ahead. These tartlets are best
filled just a few hours before serving
so fillings are still soft.
An easy way to blind bake tartlets
is to use cup cake paper cases.
One small paper case just covers
the bottom and sides of a 7.5 cm
(3 inch) tartlet mould.

◆ First prepare the custard sauce. With a swivel-bladed vegetable peeler, remove strips of zest from the lemon. Place in a medium saucepan over a medium heat with the milk and bring to the boil. Remove from the heat and leave for 5 minutes to infuse. Reheat the milk gently.

◆ Beat the egg yolks and sugar until pale and thick, 2-3 minutes. Pour about 250 ml (8 fl oz) hot milk over, beating vigorously. Return the egg yolk mixture to the pan and cook gently over a low heat until the mixture thickens; do not let it boil or it will curdle. Strain into a chilled bowl. Squeeze 30 ml (2 tbsp) juice from the lemon and stir into the sauce. Cool, stirring occasionally. Refrigerate until ready to use.

◆ Prepare the lemon curd filling. Grate the zest and squeeze the juice of the lemons into the top of a double boiler. Add the butter and sugar and stir over medium heat until the butter is melted and sugar dissolved. Lower the heat. In a bowl, lightly beat the eggs, then string into the butter mixture. Cook over a low heat, stirring until the mixture thickens, about 15 minutes. Pour (or strain if you do not want the lemon zest) into a bowl. Cool, stirring occasionally. Refrigerate to thicken.

◆ Prepare the pastry. Place the flour, sugar and salt into a food processor fitted with a metal blade. Process to blend. Add the butter and process for 15-20 seconds, until the mixture resembles coarse crumbs. In a bowl, beat the egg yolk with the vanilla essence and water. With the food processor running, pour the egg yolk mixture through the feed tube just until the dough begins to stick together; do not allow the dough to form a ball or the pastry will be tough. If the dough appears too dry add 15–30 ml (1-2 tbsp) more cold water.

◆ Place a piece of clingfilm on a work surface. Turn the dough out on to the clingfilm. Use the clingfilm to help shape the dough into a flat disc. Wrap tightly and refrigerate for at least 30 minutes.

◆ Lightly butter 12 7.5 cm (3 inch) tartlet tins (if possible, with removable bases). On a lightly floured surface, roll out the dough to an oblong shape slightly more than 3 mm (⅛ inch) thick. Using a 10 cm (4 inch) fluted cutter, cut out 12 circles and press each one on to the bottom and sides of the tartlet tins. Prick the bottom of the dough with a fork. Place the tins on a large baking sheet and refrigerate for 30 minutes.

◆ Preheat the oven to 190°C (375°F, Gas Mark 5). Cut out 12 12.5 cm (5 inch) circles of foil and line each tin; fill with dry beans or rice. Bake for 5-8 minutes; remove the foil with the beans and bake for 5 minutes longer, until golden. Transfer the tartlets to a wire rack to cool.

◆ Prepare the chocolate filling. In a saucepan over a medium heat, bring the cream to the boil. Remove from the heat and stir in the chocolate until melted and smooth. Beat in the butter and leave to cool slightly.

◆ Spoon an equal amount of chocolate filling into each tartlet. Refrigerate for 10 minutes.

◆ On to each chocolate-filled tartlet, spoon a layer of lemon curd. Set aside, but do not refrigerate or the chocolate layer will be too firm.

◆ Spoon a little custard on to dessert plates. Remove the tartlets from the tins and place in the centre of the plates. Decorate each tartlet with a chocolate triangle. If you like, spoon melted chocolate into a paper cone, and make drops of chocolate circles. Draw a cocktail stick or skewer through the circles to marble into the custard or make a heart motif.

Mocha-Fudge Pie with Coffee Custard Cream

SERVES 10

100 g (4 oz) plain chocolate, chopped
100 g (4 oz) butter, cut into pieces
4 eggs
1 tbsp golden syrup
100 g (4 oz) sugar
1 tbsp instant coffee powder, dissolved
in 15-30 ml (1-2 tbsp) hot water
1 tsp ground cinnamon
45 ml (3 tbsp) milk

Coffee custard cream
750 ml (1¼ pt) milk
1 tbsp instant coffee powder, dissolved
in 15-30 ml (1-2 tbsp) hot water
175 g (6 oz) sugar
6 egg yolks
2 tsp cornflour
30 ml (2 tbsp) coffee-flavour liqueur

To decorate
whipped cream
chocolate coffee beans

◆ Preheat the oven to 180°C (350°F, Gas Mark 4). Lightly grease a 23 cm (9 inch) pie dish, 4 cm (1½ inch) deep.
◆ In a saucepan over a low heat, melt the chocolate and butter, stirring until smooth. Set aside.
◆ In a bowl, beat the eggs lightly. Blend in the golden syrup, sugar, dissolved coffee powder, cinnamon and milk. Stir in the chocolate mixture until well blended. Place the pie dish on a baking sheet. Pour the chocolate mixture into the pie dish.
◆ Bake for 20-25 minutes, or until the edge is set but the centre is still almost liquid. Transfer to a wire rack to cool completely; the top may crack slightly.
◆ Prepare the custard. In a saucepan over medium heat, bring the milk and dissolved coffee powder to the boil. In a bowl, beat the sugar and egg yolks until pale and thick, 3-5 minutes. Stir in the cornflour just until blended.

◆ Slowly pour about 250 ml (8 fl oz) hot milk into the yolks, stirring constantly. Return the yolk mixture to the pan and cook over a low heat, stirring constantly, until the sauce thickens, 5-8 minutes; *do not allow the sauce to boil or it will curdle.* Strain into a *chilled* bowl and stir until slightly cool. Stir in the coffee-flavour liqueur and cool completely. Refrigerate until ready to serve.
◆ To serve, place a spoonful of custard on a dessert plate and place a slice of tart on the pool of custard. If you like, garnish with softly whipped cream and chocolate coffee beans.

White Chocolate and Banana Cream Tart

SERVES 8

175 g (6 oz) plain flour
65 g (2½ oz) shredded sweetened coconut
100 g (4 oz) butter, softened
2 tbsp caster sugar
2 egg yolks
2.5 ml (½ tsp) almond essence

White chocolate custard
150 g (5 oz) good-quality white chocolate, chopped
120 ml (4 fl oz) double cream
40 g (1½ oz) cornflour
1 tbsp plain flour
75 g (3 oz) sugar
450 ml (16 fl oz) milk
5 egg yolks
600 ml (1 pt) whipping cream
2.5 ml (½ tsp) almond essence
3 very ripe bananas
50 g (2 oz) chopped almonds, toasted

◆ Prepare the pastry. With an electric mixer at low speed, combine the flour, coconut, butter, sugar, egg yolks and almond essence until blended.

◆ Press the dough on to the bottom and sides of a lightly buttered tart tin with removable base. Prick the dough with a fork. Refrigerate for 30 minutes.

◆ Preheat the oven to 180°C (350°F, Gas Mark 4). Line the tart shell with foil or greaseproof paper; fill with dry beans or rice. Bake for 10 minutes. Lift out the foil or paper with the beans and bake for 5-7 minutes longer, until golden. Cool on a wire rack.

◆ Prepare the custard. Melt the white chocolate with the cream, stirring until smooth. Set aside.

◆ Combine the cornflour, flour and sugar. Stir in the milk and cook until thickened and bubbling.

◆ Beat the egg yolks lightly. Slowly pour about 250 ml (8 fl oz) hot milk into the yolks, stirring constantly.

Return the egg yolk mixture to the pan and bring to a gentle boil, stirring constantly. Cook for 1-2 minutes longer. Stir in the melted chocolate until well blended. Cool to room temperature, stirring frequently to prevent a skin from forming.

◆ With an electric mixer, beat the whipping cream with the almond essence until soft peaks form. Fold about 120 ml (4 fl oz) whipped cream into the white chocolate custard.

◆ Slice the bananas and line the bottom of the pastry shell with the slices. Pour the white chocolate custard over and spread evenly. Remove the side of the tin and slide on to a plate.

◆ Pipe the remaining cream in a scroll pattern in parallel rows, 1 cm (½ inch) apart. Sprinkle the chopped toasted almonds between the rows.

Chocolate and Pine Nut Tart

SERVES 7-8

Sweet French tart pastry
175 g (6 oz) plain flour
50 g (2 oz) caster sugar
¼ tsp salt
100 g (4 oz) butter, cut into small pieces
3 egg yolks, lightly beaten
15-30 ml (1-2 tbsp) iced water

Filling
2 eggs
75 g (3 oz) sugar
zest of 1 orange, grated
15 ml (1 tbsp) orange-flavour liqueur
250 ml (8 fl oz) whipping cream
100 g (4 oz) plain chocolate, chopped
65 g (2 ½ oz) pine nuts, toasted

Glaze
1 orange
120 ml (4 fl oz) water
50 g (2 oz) sugar
15 ml (1 tbsp) cold water

◆ Prepare the pastry. In a food processor fitted with a metal blade, process the flour, sugar and salt to blend. Add the butter and process for 15-20 seconds, until the mixture resembles coarse crumbs. Add the egg yolks and using pulse action, process just until the dough begins to stick together; do not allow the dough to form a ball or the pastry will be tough. If the dough appears dry, add 30 ml (1-2 tbsp) iced water, little by little, just until the dough holds together.

◆ Turn the dough on to a lightly floured work surface and using a pastry scraper to scrape the dough, knead gently until well blended. Shape the dough into a flat disc and wrap tightly in clingfilm. Refrigerate for 4-5 hours.

◆ Lightly butter a 23 cm (9 inch), 4 cm (1½ inch) deep tart tin with a removable base. Soften the dough for 5-10 minutes at room temperature. On a well-floured surface, roll out the dough into a 27.5 cm (11 inch) circle about 5 mm (¼ inch) thick. Roll the dough loosely around the rolling pin and unroll over the tart tin; ease the dough into the tin.

◆ With floured fingers, press the overhang down slightly toward the centre, making the top edge thicker, then roll the rolling pin over the tin edge to cut off the excess dough. Press the thicker top edge against the side of the tin to form a rim about 5 mm (¼ inch) higher than the tin. Using thumb and forefinger, crimp the edge. Prick the bottom of the dough with a fork. Refrigerate for 1 hour.

◆ Preheat the oven to 200°C (400°F, Gas Mark 6). Line the tart shell with foil or greaseproof paper and fill with dry beans or rice. Bake for 5 minutes, lift out the foil or paper with the beans and bake for 5 minutes longer, just until set. Remove to a wire rack to cool slightly. Lower the oven temperature to 190°C (375°F, Gas Mark 5).

◆ In a bowl, beat together the eggs, sugar, orange zest and orange-flavour liqueur. Blend in the cream.

◆ Sprinkle chopped chocolate evenly over the bottom of the tart shell, then sprinkle pine nuts over. Place the tin on a baking sheet and gently pour the egg-and-cream mixture into the shell.

◆ Bake for 30-35 minutes, until the pastry is golden and the egg mixture is set. Transfer to a wire rack to cool for 10 minutes.

◆ Prepare the glaze. With a swivel-bladed vegetable peeler, remove thin strips of orange zest and cut into julienne strips. In a saucepan over high heat, bring the orange strips, water and sugar to the boil. Boil for 5-8 minutes, until the syrup is thickened; stir in the cold water.

◆ With a pastry brush, glaze the tart with sugar syrup and arrange the julienne orange strips over the top. Remove the side of the tin and slide the tart on to a plate. Serve the tart warm.

Chocolate Syrup Tart

SERVES 8

225 g (8 oz) plain flour
2 tbsp icing sugar
225 g (8 oz) butter
a little water
100 g (4 oz) plain chocolate
3 eggs
3 tbsp golden syrup
225 g (8 oz) sugar
5 ml (1 tsp) vanilla essence
vanilla ice cream

◆ Preheat the oven to 180°C (350°F, Gas Mark 4). Sieve the flour and icing sugar into a bowl. Rub in 150 g (5 oz) butter until the mixture resembles fine crumbs.
◆ Add enough water to mix to a stiff dough.
◆ Roll out the pastry and use to line a 23 cm (9 inch) pie dish.
◆ Put the remaining butter and the chocolate into a saucepan. Stir over gentle heat until melted and blended.
◆ Beat the eggs, syrup, sugar and vanilla essence together. Stir in the chocolate mixture.

◆ Pour the filling into the pastry case. Bake in the oven for about 40 minutes, until the top is crunchy and the filling set. (The filling should be soft inside.)
◆ Serve warm with scoops of vanilla ice cream.

Chocolate Truffle Tart

SERVES 10

100 g (4 oz) plain flour
40 g (1½ oz) cocoa powder
50 g (2 oz) caster sugar
½ tsp salt
100 g (4 oz) well-chilled butter, cut
into pieces
1 egg yolk
15-30 ml (1-2 tbsp) iced water

Truffle filling
300 ml (10 fl oz) double cream
350 g (12 oz) plain chocolate, chopped
40 g (1½ oz) butter, cut into pieces
15-30 ml (1-2 tbsp) orange-flavour
liqueur or brandy (optional)
25 g (1 oz) good-quality white
chocolate, melted

◆ First prepare the pastry. Sift the flour and cocoa powder into a bowl. In a food processor fitted with a metal blade, process the flour mixture, sugar and salt to blend. Add the butter and process for 15-20 seconds, until the mixture resembles coarse crumbs.

◆ In another bowl, lightly beat the egg yolk with the iced water. Add to the flour mixture and, using pulse action, process just until the dough begins to stick together; do not allow the dough to form into a ball or the pastry will be tough. The dough should be soft and creamy and may be difficult to handle. Place a piece of clingfilm on a work surface. Turn out the dough on to the clingfilm. Use the clingfilm to help shape the dough into a flat disc and wrap tightly. Refrigerate for 1-2 hours.

◆ Lightly grease a 23 cm (9 inch) tart tin, 4 cm (1½ inch) deep, with a removable base. Soften the dough for 5-10 minutes at room temperature. Roll out the dough between 2 sheets of greaseproof paper or clingfilm to a 27.5 cm (11 inch) circle about 5 mm (¼ inch) thick. Peel off the top sheet of greaseproof paper or clingfilm and invert the dough into the tin. Remove the bottom layer of paper or clingfilm. Press the dough on to the bottom and sides of the tin. Prick the bottom of the dough with a fork. Refrigerate for 1 hour.

◆ Preheat the oven to 190°C (375°F, Gas Mark 5). Line the tart shell with foil or greaseproof paper; fill with dried beans or rice. Bake 5-7 minutes; lift out foil or paper with the beans and bake for 5-7 minutes longer, just until set. The base of the pastry may look slightly underdone, but it will dry out. Transfer to a wire rack to cool completely.

◆ Prepare the filling. In a saucepan over a medium heat, bring the cream to the boil. Remove the pan from the heat and stir in the chocolate until melted and smooth. Stir in the butter and liqueur.

◆ Strain into the tart shell, tilting slightly to even the surface, but do not touch the surface.

◆ Spoon the melted white chocolate into a paper cone and cut the tip about 5 mm (¼ inch) in diameter. Drizzle white chocolate over the surface of the dark chocolate in an abstract design. Refrigerate for 2-3 hours, until set. To serve, leave the tart to soften slightly at room temperature, about 30 minutes.

READS

Chocolate Ring Doughnuts

MAKES ABOUT 12

225 g (8 oz) plain flour
½ tsp bicarbonate of soda
1 tsp cream of tartar
25 g (1 oz) butter
50 g (2 oz) soft brown sugar
50 g (2 oz) plain chocolate
5 ml (1 tsp) vanilla essence
1 egg, beaten
milk
oil for deep frying
caster sugar mixed with ground
cinnamon

Icing
100 g (4 oz) plain chocolate
60 ml (4 tbsp) milk and water mixed
225 g (8 oz) icing sugar, sieved

◆ Sieve the flour, bicarbonate of soda and cream of tartar into a bowl.

◆ Rub in the butter and stir in the sugar.

◆ Melt the chocolate and vanilla essence together.

◆ Pour the beaten egg and chocolate into the dry ingredients and mix to a stiff dough, adding a little milk if necessary.

◆ Knead very lightly and roll out until about 1 cm (½ inch) thick.

◆ Using a floured ring cutter (or a large and small round pastry cutter) stamp out the doughnuts. Reserve the centres.

◆ Heat the oil to 182°C (360°F) and fry the doughnuts a few at a time until golden brown. Drain and cool.

◆ Cook the doughnut centres (called doughnut "holes"). Drain. While still warm, toss in caster sugar which has cinnamon added to it. Serve the doughnut holes warm.

◆ To make the icing, melt the chocolate and liquid together. Add the icing sugar and beat well.

◆ Spread the icing over the cooled doughnut rings.

Chocolate Croissants

MAKES ABOUT 12

450 g (1 lb) strong white flour
1 tsp salt
25 g (1oz) lard
25 g (1 oz) fresh yeast
225 ml (8 fl oz) tepid water
1 egg, beaten
175 g (6 oz) butter
225 g (8 oz) chocolate chips
10 ml (2 tsp) water
1 tsp sugar

◆ Sieve together the flour and salt. Rub in the lard.
◆ Blend the yeast with the water. Add the yeast liquid and egg to the flour and mix to a soft dough.
◆ Knead lightly on a floured surface for 10-15 minutes until smooth. Roll out to a strip measuring 51 x 20 cm (20 x 8 inches).
◆ Soften the butter and divide into 3. Dot 1 portion of the butter over two-thirds of the dough. Fold the dough in 3, folding up the unbuttered portion first. Seal the edge with a rolling pin. Wrap in clingfilm and chill.
◆ Repeat twice more, using the other 2 portions of butter. Wrap in clingfilm and chill.
◆ Roll out and fold 3 more times. Chill for at least 1 hour.

◆ Roll out to a rectangle measuring 55 x 30 cm (22 x 12 inches). Trim the edges and cut in half lengthways. Cut each strip into triangles.
◆ At the base of each triangle put a little pile of chocolate chips.
◆ Beat together the egg, water and sugar. Brush over the edges of each croissant.
◆ Roll up each croissant loosely, starting at the base and finishing with the tip underneath.
◆ Put on to a baking sheet and shape.
◆ Cover with oiled polythene and leave to rise for 20-30 minutes. Brush with egg glaze.
◆ Preheat the oven to 320°C (425°F, Gas Mark 7). Bake the croissants in the oven for about 20 minutes. Cool on a wire rack. Serve warm.

Chocolate Muffins

MAKES 12

225 g (8 oz) plain flour
3 tbsp unsweetened cocoa powder
50 g (2 oz) sugar
1 tsp baking powder
a pinch of salt
50 g (2 oz) raisins
1 egg, beaten
225 ml (8 fl oz) milk
50 ml (2 fl oz) corn oil

◆ Preheat the oven to 200°C (400°F, Gas Mark 6). Sieve the flour and cocoa powder into a bowl. Stir in the sugar, baking powder, salt and raisins.
◆ Beat together the egg, milk and oil.
◆ Add the liquid to the dry ingredients all at once, and mix quickly together. Do not over-mix.
◆ Spoon the mixture into 12 greased 6.5 cm (2½ inch) deep bun or muffin tins.
◆ Bake for about 20 minutes.
◆ Turn out on to a wire rack. Serve warm, split and buttered.

SWEET SUCCESS

If you need to use the same baking sheets to bake in batches, cool by running the back of the baking sheet under cold water and wiping the surface with a paper towel before regreasing.

Chocolate Caramel Pecan Bread

MAKES 9 ROLLS

225 g (8 oz) strong white flour
15 g (½ oz) fresh yeast
1 tsp sugar
120 ml (4 fl oz) tepid milk
½ tsp salt
25 g (1 oz) butter
1 egg, beaten
25 g (1 oz) butter, melted
50 g (2 oz) plain chocolate
75 g (3 oz) pecan nuts, chopped
½ tsp mixed spice
50 g (2 oz) soft brown sugar

Glaze
100 g (4 oz) plain chocolate
25 g (1 oz) butter
1 tbsp honey

◆ Sieve 50 g (2 oz) of the flour into a bowl. Add the yeast, sugar and milk and mix to a smooth batter. Leave in a warm place for 10-20 minutes or until frothy.

◆ Sieve the remaining flour with the salt into a bowl and rub into the butter. Add to the yeast batter. Stir in the egg and mix to a soft dough.

◆ Knead on a lightly floured surface for about 5 minutes until smooth. Put into a lightly oiled bowl. Cover with clingfilm and leave to rise in a warm place for about 1 hour or until double in size.

◆ Knock back the dough and knead well. Roll out to an oblong of about 30 x 23 cm (12 x 19 inches). Melt together the butter and chocolate and brush over the dough.

◆ Mix together the nuts, spice and sugar and sprinkle over the dough.

◆ Roll up lengthways, like a Swiss roll. Cut into 9 slices.

◆ Grease an 18 cm (7 inch) square cake tin. Place the slices, cut side down, in the tin. Cover with oiled clingfilm and leave to rise in a warm place for about 30 minutes.

◆ Preheat the oven to 190°C (375°F, Gas Mark 5). Remove the clingfilm and bake the bread in the oven for about 30 minutes.

◆ Turn out on to a wire rack. Melt together the chocolate, butter and honey. Drizzle over the bread while warm. Serve warm.

Danish Pastries

MAKES ABOUT 16

25 g (1 oz) fresh yeast
150 ml (¼ pt) tepid water
450 g (1 lb) plain flour
a pinch of salt
50 g (2 oz) lard
2 tbsp sugar
2 eggs, beaten
275 g (10 oz) butter

Filling
50 g (2 oz) butter
100 g (4 oz) icing sugar, sieved
75 g (3 oz) plain chocolate, melted
25 g (1 oz) toasted almonds, finely
chopped
a few drops of almond essence

Glaze
1 egg, beaten
honey

◆ Blend the yeast and water together.
◆ Sieve the flour and salt into a bowl and rub in the lard. Stir in the sugar.
◆ Add the yeast liquid and eggs to the flour and mix to a smooth elastic dough. Knead lightly. Put into a lightly oiled bowl and cover with clingfilm. Chill for 10 minutes.
◆ Soften the butter and shape into a flat oblong on greaseproof paper.
◆ Roll out the dough on a floured surface to a rectangle 3 times the size of the butter.
◆ Place the butter in the centre of the dough and fold the dough over to enclose it. Press the rolling pin firmly along the open sides.
◆ Give the dough a quarter turn and roll out to a rectangle 3 times as long as it is wide.
◆ Fold into 3. Wrap in clingfilm and chill for 10 minutes. Repeat the rolling and folding 3 more times.

◆ To make the filling, beat together the butter and icing sugar. Beat in the chocolate, almonds and almond essence. Chill.
◆ Roll out the dough thinly and cut into 7.5 cm (3 inch) squares.
◆ Put a rounded teaspoonful of filling on to the centre of each square. Bring 2 opposite corners of the dough to the centre. Either seal with beaten egg or insert a wooden cocktail stick through.
◆ Place on a greased baking sheet. Cover with greased clingfilm and leave to prove for about 30 minutes.
◆ Preheat the oven to 220°C (425°F, Gas Mark 7). Brush the dough with beaten egg. Bake for about 20 minutes.
◆ Brush with a little honey while warm.

Chocolate Waffles

SERVES 4

150 g (5 oz) plain flour
25 g (1 oz) unsweetened cocoa
powder
a pinch of salt
2 tsp baking powder
25 g (1 oz) sugar
2 eggs, separated
300 ml (½ pt) milk
50 g (2 oz) butter, melted

To serve
4 tbsp Chocolate Syrup (see page 150)
4 tbsp maple syrup
25-50 g (1-2 oz) pecan nuts, chopped

◆ Sieve together the flour, cocoa powder, salt and baking powder. Stir in the sugar.
◆ Make a well in the centre and add the egg yolks, milk and butter. Stir well together.
◆ Whisk the egg whites until stiff. Fold lightly into the batter.
◆ Pour the batter into a heated waffle iron and cook.
◆ To serve, mix together the chocolate and maple syrup and stir in the nuts. Serve the waffles immediately with the sauce poured over.

HOT DESSERTS

Banana Choc-Chip Pudding   91

Hot Chocolate Soufflé with White Chocolate

and Orange Sauce   92

Chocolate Fondue   92

Magic Chocolate Pudding   94

Baked Alaska   95

Apricot-Glazed White Chocolate Rice Pudding with

Bitter Chocolate Sauce   96

Cinnamon Chocolate Pain Perdu   98

Chocolate Upside-Down Pudding   99

Chocolate Crêpes with Pineapple and

Bitter Chocolate Sauce   100

Banana Choc-Chip Pudding

SERVES 4-5

100 g (4 oz) butter or margarine
100 g (4 oz) sugar
2 eggs, beaten
150 g (5 oz) self-raising flour
25 g (1 oz) unsweetened cocoa powder
approximately 30 ml (2 tbsp) milk
1 small banana, peeled and chopped
50 g (2 oz) chocolate chips

Sauce
175 g (6 oz) soft brown sugar
25 g (1 oz) butter
2 tbsp golden syrup
4 tbsp single cream

◆ Cream the butter or margarine and sugar together until light and fluffy.
◆ Gradually add the eggs, beating well between each addition.
◆ Sieve together the flour and cocoa, and fold into the egg mixture. Add enough milk to give a soft dropping consistency.
◆ Stir in the banana and chocolate chips.
◆ Turn the mixture into a greased 900 ml (1½ pt) pudding basin. Cover with greased greaseproof paper and foil with a central pleat in each. Secure with string. Steam for 1½ hours.

◆ To make the sauce, put all the ingredients into a saucepan and bring to the boil, stirring.
◆ Turn out the pudding and serve with warm sauce.

Hot Chocolate Soufflé with White Chocolate and Orange Sauce

SERVES 6

granulated sugar for sprinkling dish
100 g (4 oz) plain chocolate, chopped
50 g (2 oz) unsalted butter, cut into
pieces
4 eggs, separated
30 ml (2 tbsp) orange-flavour liqueur
1.5 ml (¼ tsp) cream of tartar
2 tbsp sugar
icing sugar for dusting

Chocolate and orange sauce
75 g (3 oz) good-quality white
chocolate, chopped
75 ml (2½ fl oz) whipping cream
30 ml (2 tbsp) orange-flavour liqueur
30 ml (2 tbsp) orange juice

◆ Preheat the oven to 240°C (475°F, Gas Mark 9). Generously butter a 1 litre (1¾ pt) soufflé dish. Refrigerate for 5 minutes to set the butter, then rebutter the dish. Lightly sprinkle the base and sides of the dish with sugar, then shake out any excess.

◆ Melt the chocolate and butter. Remove from the heat. Beat in the egg yolks and orange-flavour liqueur. Set aside to cool slightly, stirring occasionally.

◆ With an electric mixer, beat the egg whites and cream of tartar together until stiff peaks form. Sprinkle the sugar over and continue beating for 1 minute, until the sugar is incorporated and the whites are glossy.

◆ Fold the whites into the cooled chocolate mixture. Do not overwork the mixture. Pour into the prepared dish.

◆ Place on a baking sheet and bake for 5 minutes. Reduce the oven temperature to 220°C (425°F, Gas Mark 7) and bake for 10-12 minutes longer. The top of the soufflé should be set but the soufflé should jiggle when the baking sheet is moved; it should remain soft in the centre.

◆ Meanwhile, prepare the sauce. Melt the chocolate with the cream, stirring frequently until smooth. Stir in the orange-flavour liqueur and orange juice. Strain into a sauceboat and set aside to keep warm.

◆ To serve, dust the top of the soufflé with icing sugar. Transfer from the baking sheet to the prepared serving plate. Serve immediately; pass the sauce separately.

RIGHT *Hot Chocolate Soufflé with White Chocolate and Orange Sauce*

Chocolate Fondue

SERVES 4-6

225 g (8 oz) plain chocolate
225 g (8 oz) milk chocolate
250 ml (8 fl oz) single cream
45 ml (3 tbsp) Kahlua or Tia Maria

◆ Break the chocolate into very small pieces and put into a heavy-based saucepan. Add the cream and melt slowly over a low heat, stirring constantly.

◆ Immediately before serving, stir in the liqueur.

◆ Small chunks of Madeira or other loaf cake, marshmallows, macaroons, whole strawberries, cherries, chunks of banana, pineapple and apple all make tasty dippers.

Magic Chocolate Pudding

SERVES 4-5

100 g (4 oz) self-raising flour, sieved
50 g (2 oz) sugar
2 tbsp unsweetened cocoa powder,
sieved
50 g (2 oz) walnuts, chopped
50 g (2 oz) butter, melted
150 ml (¼ pt) milk
a few drops of vanilla essence

Sauce
150 g (5 oz) soft brown sugar
2 tbsp unsweetened cocoa powder,
sieved
210 ml (¼ pt + 4 tbsp) boiling water

◆ Preheat the oven to 180°C (350°F, Gas Mark 4). To make the sponge, put the dry ingredients into a bowl. Add the butter, milk and vanilla essence and mix to form a thick batter.
◆ Pour the mixture into a buttered 900 ml (1½ pt) ovenproof dish.
◆ To make the sauce, mix together the brown sugar, cocoa powder and boiling water. Pour this sauce over the batter.
◆ Bake in the oven for about 40 minutes. During cooking the chocolate sponge rises to the top, and a chocolate fudge sauce forms underneath.
◆ Serve with vanilla ice cream.

Baked Alaska

SERVES 6-8

900 ml (1½ pt) chocolate ice cream
3 eggs
75 g (3 oz) sugar
65 g (2½ oz) plain flour
2 tbsp unsweetened cocoa powder
approximately 225 g (8 oz) fruit
(strawberries, bananas, raspberries or
cherries)
60 ml (4 tbsp) Marsala or sweet sherry
4 egg whites
225 g (8 oz) sugar

◆ Pack the ice cream into a 450 g (1 lb) loaf tin lined with greaseproof paper. Freeze overnight.

◆ Preheat the oven to 200°C (400°F, Gas Mark 6). Put the eggs and sugar into a bowl and whisk until thick and creamy, and the whisk leaves a trail.

◆ Sieve the flour and cocoa and fold gently into the mixture.

◆ Turn into a greased and lined 23 cm (9 inch) tin. Bake in the oven for 12-15 minutes. Cool and remove the lining.

◆ Prepare the fruit by slicing it and removing stones if necessary. Put into a bowl with the Marsala or sherry.

◆ Whisk the egg whites until stiff. Whisk in the sugar a little at a time. Spoon the meringue into a piping bag fitted with a large star nozzle.

◆ Trim the edges of the sponge, then cut 2.5 cm (1 inch) strips from 2 sides of the cake to make an oblong slightly larger than the ice cream block.

◆ Preheat the oven to 230°C (450°F, Gas Mark 8). Put the sponge on an ovenproof serving dish. Spoon the fruit and juices over the sponge.

◆ Remove the ice cream from the freezer and turn it on to the sponge. Remove the paper.

◆ Quickly pipe the meringue decoratively over the ice cream, covering it completely.

◆ Bake in the oven for 3-5 minutes until lightly browned. Cut into slices and serve immediately.

Apricot-Glazed White Chocolate Rice Pudding with Bitter Chocolate Sauce

SERVES 10

100 g (4 oz) sultanas
45 ml (3 tbsp) hot water
30 ml (2 tbsp) apricot brandy or orange-flavour liqueur
150 g (5 oz) medium- or long-grain white rice
350 ml (12 fl oz) milk
250 ml (8 fl oz) water
25 g (1 oz) butter
100 g (4 oz) sugar
175 g (6 oz) good-quality white chocolate, chopped
3 eggs
475 ml (16 fl oz) double cream
10 ml (2 tsp) vanilla essence
1 tsp ground cinnamon
½ tsp grated nutmeg

Apricot glaze
120 ml (4 fl oz) apricot jam
15 ml (1 tbsp) orange juice or water
15 ml (1 tbsp) apricot brandy or orange-flavour liqueur

Bitter chocolate sauce
175 ml (6 fl oz) double cream
175 ml (6 fl oz) apricot jam
175 g (6 fl oz) bittersweet chocolate, chopped
30 ml (2 tbsp) apricot brandy or orange-flavour liqueur

◆ In a bowl, combine the sultanas, hot water and apricot brandy. Leave to stand for at least 2 hours.

◆ In a heavy-based saucepan, combine the rice, 250 ml (8 fl oz) milk, water, butter and 50 g (2 oz) sugar. Bring to the boil, stirring occasionally. Reduce the heat, cover and simmer for 18-20 minutes, just until liquid is absorbed.

◆ Meanwhile, preheat the oven to 150°C (300°F, Gas Mark 2). Butter a 1.5-2 litre (2½-3½ pt) shallow baking dish or soufflé dish and set aside. In a saucepan over a low heat, melt the chocolate with the remaining milk, stirring frequently until smooth. Remove from the heat. In a large bowl, lightly beat the eggs, remaining sugar, cream, vanilla essence, cinnamon and nutmeg. Slowly beat in the melted chocolate until well blended. Stir in the sultanas and any liquid. Stir the egg mixture into the cooked rice mixture until well blended, then pour into the baking dish. Cover with foil.

◆ Set the baking dish into a roasting tin. Fill the tin with hot water to about halfway up the side of the dish. Bake for 30 minutes, uncover and bake for 15-20 minutes longer, until a knife inserted 5 cm (2 inches) from the edge of the dish comes out clean; the centre should remain slightly moist. Run a sharp knife around the edge of the dish to loosen the pudding from the edge and prevent the centre from splitting. Leave to cool for 1 hour.

◆ Meanwhile, prepare the glaze. In a saucepan over a medium heat, melt the apricot jam with the orange juice and apricot brandy or liqueur, stirring until smooth. Gently spoon over the top of the pudding to glaze.

◆ Prepare the chocolate sauce. In a saucepan over a low heat, bring the cream and apricot jam to a boil. Remove from the heat and stir in the chocolate, stirring until melted and smooth. Press through a sieve and stir in the apricot brandy or liqueur; keep warm. Serve with the glazed rice pudding.

SWEET SUCCESS

This pudding can be made in individual moulds and unmoulded for a more elegant presentation. Butter 10 150 ml (5 fl oz) custard cups or ramekins and line the base of each with greaseproof paper. Butter the paper. Bake for 3-5 minutes less than for the above recipe. Cool the puddings for at least 1 hour; do not glaze. Unmould each pudding on to a plate, remove the paper and top with a little warm glaze; spread evenly. Pour over a little chocolate sauce and serve the remainder separately.

Cinnamon Chocolate Pain Perdu

SERVES 4-6

75-100 g (3-4 oz) butter
12-14 slices French bread
175 g (6 oz) plain chocolate
600 ml (1 pt) milk
2 eggs
2 egg yolks
1 tsp ground cinnamon
50 g (2 oz) sugar
icing sugar

◆ Preheat the oven to 190°C (375°F, Gas Mark 5). Butter the slices of bread on both sides. Place on a baking tray and bake in the oven for about 5 minutes or until lightly golden. Turn over and bake on the other side until golden, about 2-5 minutes.

◆ Melt the chocolate.

◆ Bring the milk almost to boiling point. Remove from the heat and whisk into the chocolate.

◆ Beat together the eggs, egg yolks, cinnamon and sugar. Pour on the chocolate milk and whisk well.

◆ Arrange the French bread in a large shallow baking dish. Strain the chocolate custard over the bread.

◆ Put the dish into a roasting tin and pour in boiling water to come halfway up the side of the baking dish.

◆ Cook in the oven for 30-40 minutes until lightly set.

◆ Dredge with icing sugar and serve with single cream.

Chocolate Upside-Down Pudding

SERVES 6

100 g (4 oz) Demerara sugar
50 g (2 oz) butter
4 pineapple rings
6 walnut halves
2 eggs, separated
25 g (1 oz) butter, melted
100 g (4 oz) soft brown sugar
100 g (4 oz) self-raising flour
25 g (1 oz) unsweetened cocoa powder

◆ Preheat the oven to 180°C (350°F, Gas Mark 4). Grease a 20 cm (8 inch) cake tin.
◆ Cream together the sugar and butter and spread over the base of the tin. Arrange the pineapple rings on the base, with a walnut in the centre of each.
◆ Beat together the egg yolks and butter until creamy.
◆ Whisk the egg whites until stiff. Fold in the sugar and egg yolk mixture.

◆ Sieve together the flour and cocoa and fold in carefully. Pour over the fruit and spread evenly.
◆ Bake in the oven for 30 minutes.
◆ Carefully turn out on to a serving dish and serve with pouring custard or single cream.

Chocolate Crêpes with Pineapple and Bitter Chocolate Sauce

MAKES 12

45 g (1¼ oz) plain flour
1 tbsp cocoa powder
1 tsp sugar
¼ tsp salt
2 eggs
175 ml (6 fl oz) milk
25 g (1 oz) unsalted butter, melted plus
extra for reheating crêpes
5 ml (1 tsp) vanilla essence
vegetable oil for greasing

Pineapple filling
25 g (1 oz) unsalted butter
1 pineapple, peeled, cored and cut into
1 cm (½ inch) pieces or 450 g (1 lb)
can pineapple pieces in juice, drained
½ tsp ground cinnamon
60 ml (2 fl oz) natural maple syrup
50 g (2 oz) plain or milk chocolate
chips
50 g (2 oz) macadamia nuts, chopped
and toasted

Chocolate sauce
100 g (4 oz) plain chocolate, chopped
75 ml (2½ fl oz) water
30 ml (2 tbsp) natural maple syrup
25 g (1 oz) unsalted butter, cut into
pieces
icing sugar for dusting
fresh cranberries or raspberries and
mint leaves for decoration

◆ Into a bowl, sift the flour, cocoa powder, sugar and salt. Mix to blend; make a well in the centre.

◆ In another bowl, lightly beat the eggs with the milk. Gradually add to the well in the centre of the flour mixture. Using a whisk, blend in the flour from the sides of the bowl to form a paste, then a batter; beat until smooth. Stir in the melted butter and vanilla essence and strain into another bowl. Leave to stand for 1 hour.

◆ With a pastry brush, brush the bottom of a 17.5 or 20 cm (7 or 8 inch) crêpe pan with a little vegetable oil. Heat the pan over a medium heat. Stir the batter (if the batter is too thick, stir in a little milk or water; it should be thin). Fill a 60 ml (2 fl oz) measure or small ladle three-quarters full with batter, then pour into the hot pan. Quickly tilt and rotate pan to cover the bottom of the pan with a thin layer of batter. Cook over a medium-high heat for 1-2 minutes, until the top is set and the bottom is golden. With a palette knife, loosen the edge of the crêpe from the pan, turn over and cook for 30-45 seconds, just until set. Turn out on to a plate.

◆ Continue making crêpes, stirring the batter occasionally and brushing the pan lightly with oil. (A non-stick pan is ideal and does not need additional greasing.) Stack crêpes with sheets of greaseproof paper between each. Set aside.

◆ Prepare the filling. In a large frying pan over medium-high heat, melt the butter until sizzling. Add the pineapple pieces and sauté until golden, 3-4 minutes. Sprinkle with cinnamon and stir in the maple syrup. Cook for 1-2 minutes longer, until the pineapple is lightly coated with syrup and the liquid has evaporated. Remove from the heat.

◆ Lay a crêpe on a plate or work surface, bottom side down. Spoon a little pineapple mixture on to the top half of the crêpe. Sprinkle over a few chocolate chips and macadamia nuts. Fold the bottom half over, then fold into quarters. Continue using all the crêpes, pineapple filling, chocolate chips and nuts. Set each one on a buttered baking sheet and cover tightly with foil until ready to serve.

◆ Prepare the chocolate sauce. In a medium saucepan over a low heat, melt the chocolate with water and maple syrup, stirring frequently until smooth and well blended. Stir in the butter. Keep warm.

◆ Preheat the oven to 190°C (375°F, Gas Mark 5). Uncover the crêpes, brush the top of each with melted butter and re-cover tightly. Bake for 5 minutes just until heated through. Place on a dessert plate or individual plates. Dust with icing sugar and decorate with fresh cranberries or raspberries and mint leaves. Serve the chocolate sauce separately.

COLD DESSERTS

Chocolate Mousse

SERVES 4-6

175 g (6 oz) plain chocolate
2 tbsp honey
3 eggs, separated
15 g (½ oz) powdered gelatine
45 ml (3 tbsp) hot water
150 ml (¼ pt) double cream

To serve
whipped cream
sliced bananas

◆ Put the chocolate and honey into a bowl over a pan of hot water and melt.
◆ Stir in the egg yolks and beat until smooth. Remove from the heat.
◆ Dissolve the gelatine in the water. Stir into the chocolate mixture. Chill until the mixture is the consistency of unbeaten egg white.
◆ Whip the cream until thick, but not stiff. Fold into the chocolate mixture.
◆ Whisk the egg whites until stiff and fold them into the chocolate mixture.

◆ Pour into a 1 litre (1¾ pt) mould. Chill until set.
◆ Unmould on to a serving dish. Pipe whipped cream round the base and decorate with banana slices.

Fruited White Chocolate Bavarian Creams with Passion Fruit and Chocolate Sauces

SERVES 8

vegetable oil for moulds
325 ml (11 fl oz) whipping cream
100 g (4 oz) good-quality white chocolate, chopped
2 tsp powdered gelatine
60 ml (2 fl oz) water
450 ml (16 fl oz) milk
4 egg yolks
50 g (2 oz) sugar
30 ml (2 tbsp) orange-flavour liqueur

Passion fruit sauce
6 very ripe passion fruit
60 ml (2 fl oz) orange juice
2 tbsp sugar or to taste
1 tsp cornflour, dissolved in
5 ml (1 tsp) water
15 ml (1 tbsp) orange-flavour liqueur

Chocolate liqueur sauce
225 g (8 oz) bittersweet chocolate, chopped
50 g (2 oz) unsalted butter, cut into pieces
175 ml (6 fl oz) water
30-45 ml (2-3 tbsp) chocolate-flavour liqueur

To decorate
grated chocolate
fresh mint sprigs

◆ Lightly oil 8 heart-shaped or other moulds. In a saucepan over low heat, bring 150 ml (5 fl oz) cream to the boil. Add the white chocolate all at once, stirring until smooth. Set aside.

◆ Sprinkle the gelatine over the water in a bowl; leave to stand and soften.

◆ In a saucepan over a medium heat, bring the milk to the boil. In a bowl with a hand-held electric mixer, beat the egg yolks and sugar until thick and pale, 2-3 minutes. Reduce the mixer to the lowest speed, gradually beat in the milk, then return the custard mixture to the saucepan.

◆ Cook the custard over a medium heat, stirring constantly with a wooden spoon until the mixture thickens and coats the back of the spoon; do not boil or the custard will curdle. Remove from the heat and stir in the softened gelatine until dissolved, then stir into the chocolate mixture. Strain the custard into a large chilled bowl. Stir in the orange-flavour liqueur and refrigerate for about 20 minutes, until the mixture begins to thicken.

◆ In a bowl, with an electric mixer, beat the remaining cream until soft peaks form. Gently fold into the thickening gelatine-custard mixture. Spoon an equal amount into each mould. Place the moulds on a baking sheet and refrigerate for 2 hours, or until set. Cover all the moulds with clingfilm and refrigerate for several hours.

◆ Prepare the passion fruit sauce. Halve the passion fruit crosswise. Scoop the juice and seeds into a saucepan. Stir in the orange juice, sugar and dissolved cornflour. Bring to the boil, then simmer for 1-2 minutes, until the sauce thickens. Remove from the heat; cool slightly. Stir in the orange-flavour liqueur. Pour into a sauceboat.

◆ Prepare the chocolate sauce. In a saucepan over a medium heat, melt the chocolate and butter with water, stirring frequently until smooth. Remove from the heat and cool slightly. Stir in the chocolate-flavour liqueur and strain into a sauceboat.

◆ To serve, unmould the desserts on to plates at least 30 minutes before serving to soften slightly. Fill a pie dish with hot water. Run a knife around the edge of each mould and dip into the hot water for 5-7 seconds. Dry the bottom of the mould; quickly cover the dessert with a plate. Invert the mould on to the plate giving a firm shake; carefully remove the mould.

◆ Spoon a little of each sauce around each heart-shaped Bavarian cream. Decorate with grated chocolate and fresh mint.

Chocolate Tiramisù

SERVES 14-16

Chocolate sponge fingers

75 g (3 oz) plain flour
25 g (1 oz) cocoa powder
1 tbsp instant coffee powder
¼ tsp salt
4 eggs, separated
100 g (4 oz) caster sugar
10 ml (2 tsp) vanilla essence
¼ tsp cream of tartar
icing sugar for dusting

Chocolate mascarpone filling

490 g (17½ oz) container mascarpone
cheese, at room temperature
75 g (3 oz) icing sugar, sifted
350 ml (12 fl oz) freshly brewed
instant coffee
600 ml (1 pt) double cream
175 g (6 oz) plain chocolate, melted
and cooled
90 ml (6 tbsp) coffee-flavour liqueur
50 g (2 oz) plain chocolate, grated
30 ml (2 tbsp) chocolate-flavour
liqueur

To serve

cocoa powder for dusting
whipped cream (optional)

SWEET SUCCESS

Mascarpone is an Italian cream cheese with a smooth creamy texture and soft, sweet flavour. It is available from supermarkets and speciality stores. A quicker version of this recipe can be made using about 200 g (7 oz) bought sponge fingers. In either case, make this dessert at least 1 day ahead to allow the mixture to set firm and the flavours to mingle.

◆ Prepare the sponge fingers. Grease 2 large baking sheets and line with greaseproof paper. Grease and lightly flour the paper. In a bowl, sift together twice the flour, cocoa powder, coffee powder and salt. Mix well and set aside.

◆ In another bowl, with an electric mixer, beat the egg yolks with 50 g (2 oz) sugar until thick and pale, 2-3 minutes. Beat in the vanilla essence.

◆ In a large bowl, with an electric mixer and cleaned beaters, beat the egg whites and cream of tartar until stiff peaks form. Sprinkle over the remaining sugar, 2 tbsp at a time, beating well after each addition.

◆ Fold 1 spoonful of egg whites into the egg-yolk mixture to lighten, then fold in remaining egg whites. Sift the flour mixture over and fold into the egg mixture, but do not overwork the mixture. Spoon the batter into a large piping bag fitted with a medium (about 1 cm/½ inch) plain nozzle. Pipe the batter into about 30 12.5 cm (5 inch) or 24 10 cm (4 inch) sponge fingers. Dust with icing sugar.

◆ Bake for 12-15 minutes, until set and tops feel firm when touched with a fingertip. Transfer to a wire rack to cool on baking sheets for 10 minutes. With a wide spatula, transfer the sponge fingers to wire racks to cool.

◆ With a hand-held electric mixer at low speed, beat the mascarpone cheese with the icing sugar just until smooth. Gradually beat in 60 ml (2 fl oz) coffee; do not overbeat.

◆ In another bowl, with an electric mixer, beat the cream until soft peaks form. Gently fold the cream into the mascarpone mixture. Divide the mixture in half. Fold the melted chocolate and 30 ml (2 tbsp) coffee-flavour liqueur into half until blended. Fold the grated chocolate and chocolate-flavour liqueur into the remaining mascarpone mixture. Set both mixtures aside.

◆ In a bowl or pie dish wide enough to hold the sponge fingers, combine half the remaining instant coffee with 30 ml (2 tbsp) coffee-flavour liqueur. Quickly dip side of a sponge finger into the coffee mixture and place it dry-side down in a 32.5 x 23 cm (13 x 9 inch) baking dish; do not let the sponge fingers get too soggy or they may fall apart. Continue with about half the sponge fingers (you will need enough for 2 layers) to form a fairly close layer with not much space between each sponge finger. Drizzle over the remaining coffee mixture. Place the remaining coffee and coffee-flavour liqueur in the pie dish.

◆ Pour the chocolate-mascarpone mixture over the bottom layer of sponge fingers, smoothing the chocolate mixture. Layer the remaining sponge fingers over the chocolate mixture, dipping them into the coffee mixture 1 at a time. Drizzle over any remaining coffee mixture. Pour the grated chocolate-mascarpone mixture over this layer and smooth the top, leaving no spaces between filling and sides of dish. Cover the dish tightly and refrigerate overnight. Dust the top with cocoa powder before serving. If you like, decorate with extra whipped cream.

White Chocolate Fruit Fools in Chocolate Cups

SERVES 12

12 chocolate cups (see page 18)

Mango purée
1 mango, peeled and cut into cubes,
with 4 cubes reserved for decoration
grated zest and juice of ½ orange
5 ml (1 tsp) lemon juice or to taste
1 tbsp sugar or to taste

Kiwi fruit purée
3 kiwi fruit, peeled and sliced, with 4
slices reserved for decoration
grated zest of 1 lime with 5-10 ml
(1-2 tsp) juice
1 tbsp sugar or to taste

Cranberry-raspberry purée
100 g (4 oz) fresh raspberries with
berries reserved for garnish
15 ml (1 tbsp) lemon juice
1 tsp sugar or to taste
225 g (8 oz) can cranberry sauce

White chocolate mousse
100 g (4 oz) good-quality white
chocolate, chopped
60 ml (2 fl oz) milk
15 ml (1 tbsp) orange-flavour liqueur
300 ml (10 fl oz) double cream
2 egg whites
1.5 ml (¼ tsp) cream of tartar

◆ Prepare chocolate cups as directed on page 18, using 675 g (1½ lb) plain chocolate and 1 tbsp white vegetable fat and extra-large paper cases.

◆ Prepare the fruit purées in a food processor or blender, beginning with the lightest colour purée to avoid washing the processor after each purée. Place the mango cubes in the processor with the orange zest and juice. Process until smooth. Taste the purée and add lemon juice and sugar if necessary; this depends on the natural sweetness of the fruit. Scrape the purée into a bowl. Cover and refrigerate.

◆ Place the kiwi fruit slices into the processor with lime zest and juice. Process until smooth. Taste the purée and add more lime juice and sugar if necessary. Scrape the purée into a bowl. Cover and refrigerate.

◆ Place the raspberries, lemon juice and sugar into the food processor. Process until smooth. Press through a strainer into a bowl. Return to the food processor. Add the cranberry sauce and using the pulse action, process once or twice, just to blend, but leaving some texture to the purée. Taste the purée and add more lemon juice or sugar if necessary. Scrape the purée into small bowl. Cover and refrigerate.

◆ Prepare the mousse. In a saucepan over low heat, melt the white chocolate with the milk, stirring frequently until smooth. Remove from the heat and stir in the orange-flavour liqueur. Cool to room temperature.

◆ With a hand-held electric mixer, beat the cream until soft peaks form. Stir 1 spoonful of cream into the chocolate mixture to lighten, then fold in the remaining cream.

◆ In another bowl, with an electric mixer with clean beaters, beat egg whites and cream of tartar until stiff peaks form. Fold into the chocolate-cream mixture. (You may not want to use all the egg whites if the mousse is soft enough; this depends on the brand of chocolate used.) Divide into 3 bowls.

◆ To assemble, arrange the prepared chocolate cups on 1 large or 2 smaller baking sheets (arrange adequate refrigerator space beforehand). Spoon a little of the mango purée into 4 chocolate cups. Spoon a little of the raspberry purée into 4 chocolate cups and then the kiwi fruit purée into the remaining 4 cups. Reserve a little of each purée for topping, then fold each of the purées into one of each of the 3 bowls of mousse; do not mix well – leave swirls of purée visible for effect. Spoon each fool mixture into the appropriate chocolate cups and top each with a decorative swirl of its matching purée. Refrigerate until ready to serve. Decorate each with a berry or a cube or slice of fruit. Refrigerate for at least 30 minutes or until firm.

SWEET SUCCESS

Pretty chocolate cups can be made using brioche moulds or teacups. Line each mould or cup with a square of foil. Do not press tightly but allow it to form folds or soft pleats against the side of the mould or cup; be sure the bottom is flat. Spoon melted chocolate down the inside of the folds, using a zig-zag motion and turning the cup. This gives an uneven pleated look.

Chocolate Roulade

SERVES 6-8

175 g (6 oz) plain chocolate
5 eggs, separated
175 g (6 oz) sugar
45 ml (3 tbsp) hot water
icing sugar, sieved

Filling
425 ml (¾ pt) double cream
50 g (2 oz) icing sugar, sieved
25 g (1 oz) unsweetened cocoa powder
2 tsp instant coffee
2.5 ml (½ tsp) vanilla essence

To decorate
icing sugar
whipped cream
crystallized violets
angelica leaves

◆ Preheat the oven to 180°C (350°F, Gas Mark 4). Melt the chocolate in a bowl over a pan of hot water.
◆ Put the egg yolks into a large bowl. Add the sugar and beat well until pale and fluffy.
◆ Add the hot water to the chocolate and stir until smooth. Whisk into the egg mixture.
◆ Whisk the egg whites until stiff. Lightly fold into the chocolate mixture. Pour into a greased and lined 39 x 24 cm (15½ x 9½ inch) Swiss roll tin.
◆ Cook in the oven for 15-20 minutes, until firm.
◆ Remove from the oven. Cover with a sheet of greaseproof paper and a damp tea towel. Leave until completely cold.

◆ To make the filling put all the ingredients into a bowl. Whisk until thick. Chill.
◆ Turn the roulade on to a sheet of greaseproof paper dusted with icing sugar. Peel away the lining paper.
◆ Spread the filling over the roulade to within 2.5 cm (1 inch) of the edge. Roll up like a Swiss roll, using the greaseproof paper to help.
◆ Place seam-side down on a serving plate and chill for 1 hour before serving.
◆ To serve, dredge the roulade with icing sugar. Pipe whipped cream down the centre and decorate with crystallized violets and angelica leaves.

RIGHT *Chocolate Roulade*

Chocolate Cheesecake Cups

SERVES 6

450 g (1 lb) cream cheese
3 eggs, separated
100 g (4 oz) sugar
150 ml (¼ pt) soured cream
15 g (½ oz) powdered gelatine
60 ml (4 tbsp) water
175 g (6 oz) plain or milk chocolate, chopped
175 g (6 oz) plain chocolate
6 individual shortcrust pastry cases (approx. 7.5 cm (3 inches) diameter)
chocolate caraque (see page 18), to decorate

◆ Put the cheese and egg yolks into a bowl. Add half of the sugar and beat well together.
◆ Stir in the soured cream.
◆ Dissolve the gelatine in the water.
◆ Whisk the egg whites until stiff. Whisk in the remaining sugar.
◆ Stir the gelatine into the cheese mixture.
◆ Fold the meringue and the chopped chocolate into the cheese mixture.
◆ Pour into 6 individual moulds and chill until set.
◆ Melt the chocolate and spread over the underneath and outsides of the pastry cases. Place upside down over small glasses to set.

◆ Turn out the cheesecakes and place one in each chocolate cup.
◆ Serve decorated with chocolate caraque.

Triple Chocolate Mousse Parfaits

SERVES 6

Bittersweet chocolate mousse
100 g (4 oz) bittersweet chocolate,
chopped
60 ml (2 fl oz) whipping cream
15 g (½ oz) pieces unsalted butter
2 eggs, separated
15 ml (1 tbsp) rum
pinch of cream of tartar

Milk chocolate mousse
100 g (4 oz) good-quality milk
chocolate, chopped
60 ml (2 fl oz) whipping cream
25 g (1 oz) pieces unsalted butter
2 eggs, separated
15 ml (1 tbsp) coffee-flavour liqueur
pinch of cream of tartar

White chocolate mousse
100 g (4 oz) good-quality white
chocolate, chopped
60 ml (2 fl oz) whipping cream
15 g (½ oz) pieces unsalted butter
2 eggs, separated
15 ml (1 tbsp) chocolate-flavour
liqueur
pinch of cream of tartar

To serve
90 ml (6 tbsp) chocolate sauce
60 ml (2 fl oz) whipped cream
6 chocolate coffee beans

◆ First prepare the bittersweet
chocolate mousse. In a saucepan,
melt the chocolate with cream,
stirring frequently until smooth.
Remove from the heat. Stir in the
butter and beat in the egg yolks,
1 at a time, then stir in the rum.
Allow to cool.
◆ With an electric mixer, beat the
egg whites and cream of tartar until
stiff peaks form; do not overbeat. Stir
in 1 spoonful of egg whites into the
chocolate mixture to lighten, then
fold in the remaining egg whites.

◆ Using a ladle or tablespoon,
carefully spoon an equal amount of
mousse into each of 6 sundae, parfait
or wine glasses. Do not touch the
edge of the glasses; if any of the
mixture drips, wipe the glass clean.
Place the glasses on a tray or baking
sheet and refrigerate for 1 hour, or
until set.
◆ Prepare the milk chocolate mousse
as above, then spoon equal amounts
over the bittersweet chocolate
mousse. Refrigerate for about 1 hour,
or until set.
◆ Prepare the white chocolate
mousse as above, then spoon equal
amounts over the milk chocolate
mousse. Cover each glass with clingfilm and refrigerate for 4-6 hours or
overnight, until set.
◆ To serve, spoon 15 ml (1 tbsp)
chocolate sauce over each mousse.
Spoon whipped cream into a small
piping bag fitted with a medium star
nozzle and pipe a rosette of cream on
to each mousse. Decorate with
chocolate coffee beans.

Chocolate Pots de Crème

SERVES 8

475 ml (16 fl oz) milk
100 g (4 oz) sugar
225 g (8 oz) plain or bittersweet
chocolate, chopped
15 ml (1 tbsp) vanilla essence
30 ml (2 tbsp) brandy or liqueur
7 egg yolks

To decorate
whipped cream
chopped pistachios
chocolate leaves (see page 19)

◆ Preheat the oven to 170°C (325°F, Gas Mark 3).
◆ In a saucepan, bring the milk and sugar to the boil. Add the chocolate all at once, stirring frequently until melted and smooth. Stir in the vanilla essence and brandy or liqueur.
◆ In a bowl, beat the egg yolks lightly. Slowly beat in the chocolate mixture until well blended. Strain the custard into a 2 litre (3½ pt) measuring jug or large pitcher.
◆ Place 8 120 ml (4 fl oz) *pots de crème* cups or ramekins into a shallow roasting tin. Pour an equal amount of custard into each cup. Pour enough hot water into the tin to come about halfway up the side of the cups.
◆ Bake for 30-35 minutes, until the custard is just set. Shake the pan slightly; the centre of each custard should jiggle. Alternatively, insert a knife into the side of 1 custard; the knife should come out clean. Remove the tin from the oven and transfer the cups from the tin to a heatproof surface to cool completely.

◆ Place the cooled custards on a baking sheet and cover with cling-film. Refrigerate until well chilled. (The custards can be stored for 2 days in the refrigerator.)
◆ To serve, decorate the top of each custard with a dollop or rosette of whipped cream. Sprinkle each with chopped pistachios and a chocolate leaf.

Chocolate Trifle

SERVES 6

200 g (7 oz) chocolate Swiss roll
420 g (14 oz) can apricot halves,
drained
600 ml (1 pt) Chocolate Custard (see
page 151)
300 ml (½ pt) double cream, whipped

To decorate
chocolate hearts (see page 19)
ratafia biscuits
glacé cherries, etc

◆ Cut the Swiss roll into 1 cm
(½ inch) slices and arrange over the
base and sides of a trifle dish.
◆ Arrange the drained apricots on
top.
◆ Pour the cold Chocolate Custard
over the apricots.
◆ Pipe the whipped double cream
over the top. Decorate with chocolate
hearts, ratafia biscuits, glacé cherries
etc, as desired.

RIGHT *Chocolate Trifle*

Chocolate-Glazed Chocolate Zuccotto

SERVES 8-10

1 chocolate roulade sponge
(see page 66)
120 ml (4 fl oz) Amaretto liqueur
450 g (1 lb) ricotta or mascarpone
cheese
100 g (4 oz) sugar
475 ml (16 fl oz) whipping cream
15 ml (1 tbsp) vanilla essence
175 g (6 oz) plain chocolate, melted
2 tbsp flaked almonds, toasted
and chopped
grated zest of 1 orange plus
30 ml (2 tbsp) juice
4 Amaretti biscuits, broken into
small pieces
50 g (2 oz) candied fruit, chopped

Chocolate sauce
50 g (2 oz) butter
45 ml (3 oz) golden syrup
100g (4 oz) plain chocolate, chopped
extra grated orange zest to decorate

◆ Prepare the chocolate roulade
sponge as on page 66. Line a 3 litre
(5 pt) glass bowl with clingfilm,
allowing enough to fold over the
bottom when the dessert is finished.
Cut the cake in half lengthwise. Cut
each strip into triangle-shaped pieces.
Sprinkle the cake pieces with 45 ml
(3 tbsp) Amaretto liqueur and line the
bowl with the cake pieces, leaving no
open spaces and pressing the cake
firmly against the sides of the bowl.
Reserve the remaining cake pieces to
make the bottom.
◆ If using ricotta cheese, press the
cheese through a strainer into a large
bowl. (This is not necessary for
mascarpone cheese.) Beat the cheese
and sugar until smooth.
◆ Beat the whipping cream with the
vanilla essence until soft peaks form.
Fold a spoonful of cream into the
cheese mixture to lighten, then fold
in the remaining cream. Divide the
mixture in half. Into half, fold the
melted chocolate and almonds; set
aside. Into the other half, fold in the
orange zest and juice, the remaining
Amaretto liqueur, the Amaretti
biscuits and candied fruit.

◆ Spoon the cheese and Amaretti
mixture into the cake-lined bowl to
form an even layer all around the
bowl. Spoon the chocolate mixture
into the centre and smooth the top.
Cover the top with the remaining
cake pieces and fold over the excess
clingfilm, pressing down lightly to
create a flat bottom. Refrigerate for 6-
8 hours or overnight, until very firm.
◆ Prepare the glaze. Melt the butter,
golden syrup and chocolate, stirring
frequently until smooth. Cool slightly
until thickened but still pourable.
◆ Peel back the clingfilm and
unmould on to a serving plate;
remove the clingfilm. Pour the glaze
over the top, using a palette knife to
spread it evenly and scrape excess off
the plate. Clean the plate. Refrigerate
for 5 minutes, until the chocolate is
set. Cut strips of greaseproof paper
into triangles and place over the
dessert about 4 cm (1½ inches) apart.
Dust with cocoa or icing sugar.
Decorate the top with orange zest.
Refrigerate until ready to serve.

Frozen Chocolate and Cherry Mousse Ring

SERVES 8

225 g (8 oz) plain chocolate, chopped
30 ml (2 tbsp) cherry-flavour liqueur
30 ml (2 tbsp) water
4 eggs, separated
¼ tsp cream of tartar
50 g (2 oz) sugar
175 ml (6 fl oz) whipping cream

Poached cherries
900 g (2 lb) fresh sweet cherries
1 orange
100 g (4 oz) sugar
120 ml (4 fl oz) seedless raspberry jam
or redcurrant jelly
1 tbsp cornflour, dissolved in
15 ml (1 tbsp) cold water

To serve
250 ml (8 fl oz) whipping cream
1 tbsp sugar
15 ml (1 tbsp) cherry-flavour liqueur
fresh mint leaves
chocolate-dipped cherries
(see page 137)

◆ Lightly oil a 1.1 litre (2 pt) freezerproof ring or other mould. Melt the chocolate with the cherry-flavour liqueur and water. Remove from the heat and beat in the egg yolks, 1 at a time, beating well after each addition.

◆ With an electric mixer, beat the egg whites and cream of tartar until soft peaks form. Gradually add the sugar, beating well, until the egg whites are stiff and glossy but not dry Fold a spoonful of egg whites into the chocolate mixture to lighten, then fold in the remaining egg whites.

◆ With a hand-held electric mixer, beat the cream just until soft peaks form. Fold into the chocolate mixture, then pour the mousse into the prepared mould. Cover the mould with clingfilm and freeze for 6-8 hours or overnight. (The mousse can be stored covered in the freezer for 1-2 days.)

◆ Prepare the cherries. Remove the stems and stones. Using a swivel-bladed vegetable peeler, remove the zest from the orange and squeeze the juice. Place in a saucepan with the sugar and water. Bring to the boil, then reduce the heat. Add the cherries to the poaching liquid and simmer for 7-10 minutes, until tender. Remove from the heat and leave the cherries in the poaching liquid for 3-4 hours.

◆ Using a slotted spoon, transfer the cherries from the liquid to a bowl. Add the raspberry jam and dissolved cornflour to the syrup and bring to the boil, then reduce the heat and simmer for 1-2 minutes until the syrup is thickened and coats the back of a spoon. Strain over the cherries and cool to room temperature. Refrigerate until completely chilled.

◆ To unmould the mousse, run a thin-bladed knife around the outer and inner edges of mould. Dip the mould into warm water to come about halfway up the sides of the mould for 5 seconds. Dry the bottom of the mould; quickly cover the top with a serving plate. Invert the mould on to the plate, giving a firm shake; remove the mould. Smooth the surface with a palette knife and freeze for 5 minutes to chill the surface.

◆ To serve, beat the cream, sugar and cherry-flavour liqueur until soft peaks form. Spoon one-quarter of cream into a small piping bag fitted with a medium star nozzle and pipe a decorative border around the edge of the mould; spoon the remaining cream into the centre of the mould. Decorate the outer edge with mint leaves and chocolate-dipped cherries and serve the cherries in their sauce separately.

Rich Chocolate Ice Cream

SERVES 4

225 g (8 oz) plain chocolate, chopped
475 ml (16 fl oz) half cream or milk
3 egg yolks
50 g (2 oz) sugar
350 ml (12 fl oz) double cream
15 ml (1 tbsp) vanilla essence

RIGHT *Rich Chocolate Ice Cream*

◆ In a saucepan over a low heat, melt the chocolate with 120 ml (4 fl oz) half cream or milk, stirring frequently until smooth. Remove from the heat.

◆ In a saucepan over a medium heat, bring the remaining half cream or milk to the boil. In a bowl, with a hand-held mixer, beat the egg yolks and sugar until thick and creamy, 2-3 minutes. Gradually pour the hot milk over the egg yolks, beating constantly, then return the mixture to the saucepan.

◆ Cook over medium heat until the custard thickens and lightly coats the back of a wooden spoon, stirring constantly; do not let the mixture boil or the custard will curdle. Immediately pour the melted chocolate over, stirring constantly until well blended.

◆ Pour the cold cream into a bowl and strain custard into the bowl with the cream. Blend well and cool to room temperature. Refrigerate until cold.

◆ Transfer the custard to an ice-cream maker and freeze according to the manufacturer's instructions. Leave to soften for 15-20 minutes before serving.

VARIATIONS

White, Dark or Milk Chocolate Chunk: *Stir 225 g (8 oz) good-quality white, dark or milk chocolate, chopped, into the ice cream when removing from the ice-cream maker.*

Mocha Ice Cream: *Prepare the ice cream as directed but add 2 tbsp instant coffee powder, dissolved in 30 ml (2 tbsp) water, to the melted chocolate before adding to the custard.*

Chocolate Orange Pots

SERVES 8

175 g (6 oz) plain chocolate
zest of 1 small orange, finely grated
3 eggs, separated
30-45 ml (2-3 tbsp) Curaçao
250 ml (8 fl oz) double cream

To decorate
whipped cream
orange zest spirals
chocolate orange sticks

◆ Put the chocolate into a bowl over a pan of hot water and melt.

◆ Remove from the heat and stir in the orange zest, egg yolks and Curaçao. Stir well and leave to cool.

◆ Whip the cream until thick. Whisk the egg whites until stiff. Fold the cream and egg whites into the chocolate mixture.

◆ Pour into 8 individual pots (such as custard cups) and chill well.

◆ To serve, top with a spoonful of softly whipped cream and decorate with orange zest spirals and chocolate sticks.

Profiteroles

SERVES 6

50 g (2 oz) unsalted butter
150 ml (¼ pt) water
65 g (2½ oz) plain flour
2 eggs, beaten

Filling
300 ml (½ pt) double cream
25 g (1 oz) icing sugar, sieved
a little Grand Marnier
2 tsp finely-grated orange zest

Chocolate sauce
100 g (4 oz) plain chocolate
30 ml (2 tbsp) orange juice
50 g (2 oz) icing sugar
25 g (1 oz) butter

◆ Melt the butter in a pan with the water.
◆ Bring to the boil and immediately tip in the flour. Beat well until the mixture forms a ball that comes cleanly away from the pan. Leave to cool.
◆ Preheat the oven to 200°C (400°F, Gas Mark 6). Beat or whisk the eggs into the mixture, a little at a time. Continue beating until the mixture is smooth and glossy.
◆ Put the mixture into a piping bag fitted with a 1 cm (½ inch) plain nozzle. Pipe about 24 small balls on to a greased and floured baking sheet.
◆ Bake in the oven for 15-20 minutes until well risen and golden brown. A

few minutes before removing from the oven, pierce them with a sharp knife to release the steam. Cool on a wire rack.
◆ To make the filling, whisk the cream until stiff. Stir in the icing sugar, Grand Marnier and orange zest. Put the cream in a piping bag fitted with a small nozzle and pipe the cream into the choux buns through the slits.
◆ To make the sauce, put all the ingredients into a bowl over a pan of hot water and heat until melted. Stir well together.
◆ Pile the profiteroles on a serving dish and just before serving, pour over the warm sauce.

Charlotte Louise

SERVES 8

18-20 sponge fingers
175 g (6 oz) unsalted butter
75 g (3 oz) sugar
175 g (6 oz) plain chocolate
100 g (4 oz) ground almonds
300 ml (½ pt) double cream
2.5 ml (½ tsp) almond essence

To decorate
whipped cream
pistachio nuts
crystallized violets or roses
satin ribbon

◆ Cut a round of greaseproof paper to fit the base of a 1.4 litre (2½ pt) charlotte mould. Oil it lightly and place in the mould.

◆ Line the sides of the mould with the sponge fingers.

◆ Cream the butter and sugar together until light and fluffy.

◆ Melt the chocolate. Cool slightly, then beat into the butter together with the ground almonds.

◆ Whip the cream until thick, but not stiff. Add the almond essence. Fold into the chocolate mixture and mix well.

◆ Spoon the mixture into the lined mould. Press in firmly. Chill well.

◆ Turn out on to a plate. Remove the paper and pipe with whipped cream. Decorate with pistachio nuts and crystallized violets or roses. Tie a satin ribbon around the charlotte.

Chocolate Pavlova with Kiwi Fruit and Orange

SERVES 8-10

3 tbsp cocoa powder
1 tsp cornflour
4 egg whites, at room temperature
¼ tsp salt
225 g (8 oz) caster sugar
5 ml (1 tsp) cider vinegar

White chocolate cream
100 g (4 oz) good-quality white chocolate, chopped
120 ml (4 fl oz) milk
15 g (½ oz) unsalted butter, cut into pieces
250 ml (8 fl oz) double cream
2 kiwi fruit, peeled and sliced
2 oranges, segmented

To decorate
fresh mint sprigs,
wallflowers

◆ Preheat the oven to 170°C (325°F, Gas Mark 3). Place a sheet of greaseproof paper on a large baking sheet and mark a 20 cm (8 inch) circle on it using a plate or cake tin as a guide. Into a bowl, sift together the cocoa powder and cornflour; set aside.

◆ In another bowl, with an electric mixer, beat the egg whites until frothy. Add the salt and continue beating until stiff peaks form. Sprinkle in the sugar, 1 tbsp at a time, making sure each addition is well blended before adding the next, until stiff and glossy. Fold in the cocoa and cornflour mixture, then fold in the vinegar.

◆ Spoon the mixture on to the circle on the paper, spreading the meringue evenly and building up the sides higher than the centre. Bake in the centre of the oven for 45-50 minutes, until set. Turn off the oven and leave the meringue to stand in the oven 45 minutes longer; the meringue may crack or sink.

◆ Meanwhile, prepare the chocolate cream. In a saucepan over low heat, melt the chocolate with the milk, stirring until smooth. Beat in the butter and cool completely.

◆ Remove the meringue from the oven. Using a palette knife, transfer to a serving plate. Cut a circle around the centre of the meringue about 5 cm (2 inches) from the edge; this allows the centre to sink gently without pulling the edges in.

◆ When the chocolate mixture is completely cool, in a bowl, with an electric mixer, beat the cream until soft peaks form. Stir half the cream into the chocolate to lighten, then fold in the remaining cream. Spoon into centre of the meringue.

◆ Arrange the kiwi fruit and orange in the centre of the chocolate cream and decorate with fresh mint and wallflowers.

RIGHT *Chocolate Pavlova with Kiwi Fruit and Orange*

Pears and Chocolate Sauce

SERVES 6

100 g (4 oz) plain chocolate
30 ml (2 tbsp) strong black coffee
30 ml (2 tbsp) apricot jam
45 ml (3 tbsp) water
60 ml (4 tbsp) double cream
large pinch of ground cinnamon
4-8 scoops vanilla or chocolate ice cream
6 ripe pears, peeled, halved and cored
crisp biscuits (such as Langues de chat), to serve

◆ Put the chocolate, coffee, jam and water into a small heavy pan. Slowly bring to the boil, stirring constantly.

◆ Remove from the heat and stir in the cream and cinnamon.

◆ Sieve into a bowl and leave to cool.

◆ Put 1 or 2 scoops of ice cream in 6 individual serving dishes. Arrange 2 pear halves on each serving.

◆ Spoon over the chocolate sauce and serve immediately with crisp biscuits.

Chocolate and Strawberry Frozen Daquoise

SERVES 10

275 g (10 oz) sugar
2 tbsp cocoa powder, sifted
5 egg whites
¼ tsp cream of tartar
600 ml (1 pt) good-quality chocolate
ice cream
600 ml (1 pt) good-quality strawberry
ice cream
475 ml (16 fl oz) whipping cream
50 g (2 oz) sugar
30 ml (2 tbsp) raspberry-flavour
liqueur

Strawberry sauce
450 g (1 lb) frozen strawberries,
drained
15 ml (1 tbsp) lemon juice

To decorate
350 g (12 oz) fresh strawberries
10 chocolate-dipped strawberries
(see page 137)

◆ Preheat the oven to 140°C (275°F, Gas Mark 1). Line 1 large and 1 small baking sheet with greaseproof paper or foil. Using a 20 cm (8 inch) cake tin or plate as a guide, mark 2 circles on the large baking sheet and 1 circle on the small baking sheet.

◆ In a bowl, mix together 50 g (2 oz) sugar and the cocoa powder. Set aside.

◆ With an electric mixer, beat the egg whites and cream of tartar until stiff peaks form. Gradually sprinkle the remaining sugar over, a little at a time, beating well after each addition, until the egg whites are stiff and glossy. Gently fold in the cocoa and sugar mixture just until blended.

◆ Spoon one-third of the meringue mixture inside each marked circle on the baking sheets. Spread each meringue out evenly to a 20 cm (8 inch) circle, smoothing the tops and edges.

◆ Bake the meringues for 1¼ hours, until crisp and dry. Transfer to wire racks to cool for 10 minutes on baking sheets. Then remove the meringues from the greaseproof paper or foil to cool completely; the meringues can be stored in an airtight container if they are not to be used at once.

◆ Place the meringue layers on a freezerproof serving plate and freeze for 20 minutes; this makes them firmer and easier to handle while spreading the ice cream. Meanwhile, remove the chocolate and strawberry ice creams from the freezer to soften for 15-20 minutes.

◆ Remove the meringue layers and serving plate from the freezer. Place 1 meringue layer on the plate and spread with chocolate ice cream to within 1 cm (½ inch) of the edge. Cover with a second meringue layer and spread with strawberry ice cream to within 1 cm (½ inch) of the edge. Top with the third meringue layer, pressing the layers gently together. Return to the freezer for 5–6 hours or overnight.

◆ In a bowl, with a hand-held mixer, beat the cream, sugar and raspberry-flavour liqueur until soft peaks form. Remove the meringue layers from the freezer and spread the top and side with cream in a swirling or decorative pattern. Freeze until ready to serve if not using at once.

◆ For the sauce, process the strawberries in a food processor with a metal blade attached, until well blended. Press the purée through a sieve into a bowl. Stir in the lemon juice and if the sauce is too thick, thin with a little water.

◆ To serve, slice fresh strawberries lengthwise and decorate the top of the daquoise. Serve each slice with some strawberry sauce and a chocolate-dipped strawberry.

Snowball Pie

SERVES 6

225 g (8 oz) plain chocolate
50 g (2 oz) butter
75 g (3 oz) crisp rice cereal
400 ml (¾ pt) vanilla ice cream
400 ml (¾ pt) chocolate ice cream
400 ml (¾ pt) strawberry ice cream

To serve
Chocolate or Fudge Sauce
(see pages 150–151)
long shreds of coconut, toasted

◆ Melt the chocolate and butter together.
◆ Stir in the crisp rice cereal and mix well together.
◆ Press the mixture over the base and up the sides of a 20 cm (8 inch) flan dish. Place in the freezer until firm.
◆ Arrange alternate scoops of the ice cream.
◆ Pour over the sauce and sprinkle with the coconut. Serve immediately.

Chocolate Frozen Yogurt

SERVES 4-6

1.2 litres (2 pt) plain low-fat yogurt
300 g (11 oz) sugar
75 g (3 oz) cocoa powder
15 ml (1 tbsp) skimmed milk powder,
dissolved in 15-30 ml (1-2 tbsp) milk
or water

◆ In a bowl, with a wire whisk, mix together the yogurt, sugar, cocoa and dissolved skimmed milk powder until smooth and well blended and the sugar is dissolved. Refrigerate for 1 hour, until cold.

◆ Transfer the yogurt mixture to an ice-cream maker and freeze according to the manufacturer's instructions; this mixture will not freeze as hard as ice cream. Transfer to a freezerproof serving bowl or container and freeze for 3-4 hours, until firm. (Frozen yogurt can be stored in the freezer for 2-3 weeks in a freezerproof container.)

VARIATION

For mocha frozen yogurt, use coffee-flavour low-fat yogurt and add 1 tbsp instant coffee powder, or experiment with other flavours.

Fruit-Studded Chocolate Marquise with Whisky Custard Cream

SERVES 12-14

50 g (2 oz) sultanas
50 g (2 oz) chopped, stoned prunes
40 g (1½ oz) chopped, dried apricots
90 ml (3½ fl oz) whisky or apricot brandy
350 g (12 oz) plain chocolate, chopped
225 g (8 oz) unsalted butter, cut into pieces
4 eggs, separated
1.5 ml (¼ tsp) cream of tartar

Whisky custard cream
475 ml (16 fl oz) half cream
2 large eggs
100 g (4 oz) sugar
30 ml (2 tbsp) whisky or apricot brandy

RIGHT *Fruit-Studded Chocolate Marquise with Whisky Custard Cream*

◆ In a bowl, mix all the dried fruit with the whisky or brandy. Leave to stand for at least 2 hours, stirring occasionally.

◆ Line a 23 x 12.5 cm (9 x 5 inch) loaf tin with clingfilm, allowing enough to fold over the bottom when the marquise is finished.

◆ In a saucepan over low heat, melt the chocolate and butter, stirring frequently until smooth. In a bowl, with a hand-held electric mixer, beat the egg yolks until pale and thick, 3-4 minutes. Stir into the warm chocolate mixture and cook over low heat for 1 minute, stirring constantly until the mixture thickens and looks shiny. Remove from the heat and cool, stirring occasionally. Stir in the fruit and any remaining whisky or brandy.

◆ With an electric mixer, beat the egg whites and cream of tartar until stiff peaks form; do not overbeat. Stir 1 large spoonful of egg whites into the chocolate mixture to lighten, then fold in the remaining egg whites.

◆ Spoon into the tin. Chill just until firm, then fold over the excess clingfilm to cover the marquise. Refrigerate for at least 6 hours or overnight.

◆ Prepare the custard cream. In a saucepan over medium heat, bring the half cream to the boil. Remove from the heat. In a bowl, beat the eggs and sugar until well blended, about 1 minute.

◆ Pour the hot cream over and return the mixture to the saucepan over a low heat. Cook for 4-5 minutes, stirring constantly with a wooden spoon until the mixture thickens and just coats the back of the spoon; do not boil or the sauce will curdle. Strain into a chilled bowl and stir in the whisky or brandy. Refrigerate until ready to use.

◆ To serve, slide the marquise and its base on to a rectangular serving dish. Refrigerate until ready to serve. Cut into thin slices and serve with whisky custard cream.

Chocolate Hazelnut Bombe

SERVES 6-8

600 ml (1 pt) vanilla ice cream
50 g (2 oz) hazelnuts, finely chopped and toasted
600 ml (1 pt) Chocolate Ice Cream (see page 116)
30 ml (2 tbsp) dark rum

To decorate
300 ml (½ pt) double cream, whipped whole hazelnuts

◆ Put a 1.2 litre (2 pt) bombe mould or pudding basin into the freezer overnight.

◆ Soften the vanilla ice cream and mix in the hazelnuts. Line the bombe mould with the ice cream and freeze.

◆ Soften the chocolate ice cream and blend in the rum. Fill the centre of the bombe. Cover with oiled greaseproof paper and freeze.

◆ To serve, turn out the bombe on to a plate. Pipe with whipped cream and decorate with whole hazelnuts. Serve cut into wedges.

Easy Frozen Chocolate-Mint Soufflé

SERVES 6

*250 g (9 oz) plain chocolate, broken
into pieces
475 ml (16 fl oz) double cream
4 eggs, separated
45–60 ml (3-4 tbsp) mint-flavour
liqueur or
15 ml (1 tbsp) peppermint essence
1.5 ml (¼ tsp) cream of tartar
50 g (2 oz) sugar
grated chocolate for decoration*

Chocolate-dipped mint leaves
*20-24 fresh mint leaves
100 g (4 oz) plain chocolate, chopped*

◆ Prepare the chocolate-dipped leaves. Rinse the mint leaves in cold water and pat dry with paper towels. Line a baking sheet with greaseproof paper.
◆ In the top of a double boiler over a low heat, melt the chocolate, stirring frequently until smooth. Leave to cool to just below body temperature.

RIGHT *Easy Frozen Chocolate-Mint Soufflé*

Holding the stem end, dip each mint leaf about halfway into the chocolate, coating both sides, leaving excess chocolate to drip into the bowl. Place the coated leaves on a baking sheet and refrigerate; these leaves can be prepared 1-2 days ahead and kept refrigerated.
◆ Prepare a collar for the soufflé dish. Cut a piece of greaseproof paper or foil long enough to encircle the dish, allowing a 5 cm (2 inch) overlap. Fold the paper or foil in half lengthwise and wrap around the dish so the collar extends about 7.5 cm (3 inch) above the sides of the dish. Secure the paper or foil with tape or kitchen string. Lightly oil the paper collar; set the dish aside.
◆ Place the chocolate in a food processor fitted with the metal blade or in a blender.
◆ In a saucepan, bring the cream to the boil. With the food processor or blender running, slowly pour the cream over the chocolate. Continue processing or blending until smooth, scraping the side of the container once.

◆ With the machine still running, add the egg yolks, 1 at a time, processing well after each addition until well blended; the chocolate mixture will be thick and creamy. Scrape into a bowl and stir in the liqueur. Cool to room temperature; the chocolate mixture will thicken further.
◆ With an electric mixer, beat the egg whites and cream of tartar just until stiff peaks form. Add the sugar, 2 tbsp at a time, and continue beating just until the egg whites are stiff and glossy; do not overbeat.
◆ Stir 1 large spoonful of egg whites into the chocolate mixture to lighten, then gently fold in remaining egg whites. Pour into the dish and freeze overnight. (The soufflé can be prepared 2-3 days ahead.)
◆ To serve, remove the tape or string from the sides of the dish and, using a knife as a guide, carefully unwrap the paper or foil from the dish and soufflé. Press the grated chocolate on to the side of the soufflé and top with a few chocolate-coated mint leaves. Serve the remaining leaves with each portion of soufflé.

Choc-Chestnut Mont Blanc

SERVES 6-8

*50 g (2 oz) unsalted butter
25 g (1 oz) sugar
175 g (6 oz) plain chocolate, melted
350 g (12 oz) chestnut purée
15-30 ml (1-2 tbsp) sherry*

To decorate
*whipped cream
ratafia biscuits
glacé chestnuts
grated chocolate*

◆ Cream the butter and sugar together until light and fluffy.
◆ Beat in the melted chocolate.
◆ Blend in the chestnut purée and sherry.
◆ Pile the mixture into the centre of individual dessert dishes and form into mountain shapes. Chill.
◆ Spoon or pipe a capping of whipped cream on the summit. Decorate the base with ratafia biscuits and glacé chestnuts. Sprinkle with grated chocolate if you wish.

WEETMEATS

Chocolate-Dipped Caramel Apples

MAKES 12

vegetable oil
12 small apples, well scrubbed and
dried
90 g (3½ oz) pecans, walnuts or
hazelnuts, finely chopped and toasted
(optional)
175 g (6 oz) chocolate, chopped

Caramel Coating
520 ml (18 fl oz) double cream
350 ml (12 fl oz) golden syrup
40 g (1½ oz) unsalted butter,
cut into pieces
225 g (8 oz) granulated sugar
90 g (3½ oz) brown sugar
pinch of salt
15 ml (1 tbsp) vanilla essence

◆ Oil a baking sheet with the vegetable oil. Insert a wooden lollipop stick firmly into the stem end of each apple; do not use metal sticks or small pointed wooden skewers as they could be harmful to children.

◆ Prepare the caramel coating. In a heavy-based saucepan, stir the cream, syrup, butter, sugars and salt. Cook over medium heat, stirring occasionally, until the sugars dissolve and the butter is melted, about 3 minutes. Bring the mixture to the boil and cook, stirring frequently, until the caramel mixture reaches 116°C (240°F) (soft ball stage) on a sugar thermometer, about 20 minutes. Place the bottom of the saucepan in a pan of cold water to stop cooking or transfer to a small, cold saucepan. Cool to about 104°C (220°F); this will take 10-15 minutes. Stir in the vanilla essence.

◆ Holding each apple by the wooden stick, quickly dip each apple into the hot caramel, turning to coat on all sides and covering the apple completely. Scrape the bottom of the apple against the edge of the saucepan to remove the excess; place on the prepared baking sheet. If necessary, reheat the caramel slightly to thin it. Leave the apples to cool for 15-20 minutes, until the caramel hardens.

◆ If using, place the nuts in a bowl. In the top of a double boiler over a low heat, melt the chocolate, stirring frequently until smooth. Remove from the heat. Dip each caramel-coated apple about two-thirds of the way into the chocolate, allowing the excess to drip off, then drip into the nuts. Place on a greaseproof paper-lined baking sheet. Leave to set for 1 hour, until the chocolate hardens.

Meringue Mushrooms

MAKES ABOUT 8

1 egg white
50 g (2 oz) caster sugar
50 g (2 oz) plain chocolate, melted
cocoa powder, to serve

◆ Preheat the oven to 140°C (275°F, Gas Mark 1). Whisk the egg white until stiff.
◆ Whisk in the sugar a little at a time until the mixture is stiff and glossy.
◆ Put the meringue into a piping bag fitted with a 1 cm (½ inch) plain nozzle.
◆ Line a baking sheet with greaseproof paper. Pipe 6-8 small mounds of meringue about 2.5 cm (1 inch) in diameter to form the mushroom caps.

◆ Next pipe 6-8 smaller mounds, drawing each one up to a point, to represent the stalks.
◆ Bake in the oven for about 1 hour until dry and crisp. Allow to cool.
◆ Using the point of a sharp knife, make a tiny hole in the base of each mushroom cap.
◆ Spread a little melted chocolate on the underside of each cap and gently push on a stalk. Allow to set.
◆ Before serving, dust the mushrooms with a little cocoa powder.

Chocolate Fudge

MAKES ABOUT 750 G (1½ LB)

450 g (1 lb) sugar
150 ml (¼ pt) milk
100 g (4 oz) butter
175 g (6 oz) plain chocolate
50 g (2 oz) honey

◆ Put all the ingredients into a heavy-based saucepan.
◆ Stir continuously over a gentle heat until the sugar is completely dissolved.
◆ Bring to the boil and cook to the soft ball stage, 116°C (240°F).
◆ Remove from the heat and dip the base of the pan in cold water to stop further cooking.

◆ Leave for 5 minutes. Then beat the mixture with a wooden spoon until thick and creamy and beginning to "grain". Before it becomes too stiff, pour into a buttered 20 cm (8 inch) square tin. Leave to set.
◆ Using a greased knife, cut into 2.5 cm (1 inch) squares. To store the fudge, put in a tin between layers of greaseproof paper.

Chocolate Caramel Popcorn

SERVES 3-4

50 g (2 oz) brown sugar
25 g (1 oz) butter
1½ tbsp golden syrup
15 ml (1 tbsp) milk
50 g (2 oz) chocolate chips
a pinch of bicarbonate of soda
1.1 litres (2 pt) popped popcorn

◆ Preheat the oven to 150°C (300°F, Gas Mark 2). Put the sugar, butter, syrup and milk into a heavy-based saucepan.

◆ Stir over a gentle heat until the butter and sugar have melted. Bring to the boil.

◆ Boil without stirring for 2 minutes.

◆ Remove from the heat. Add the chocolate and bicarbonate of soda. Stir until the chocolate is melted.

◆ Measure the popped popcorn into a bowl. Pour over the syrup and toss well until evenly coated.

◆ Spread the mixture on a large baking sheet. Bake in the oven for about 15 minutes. Test for crispness. Bake for a further 5-10 minutes if necessary. Cool.

Chocolate Turtles

MAKES ABOUT 30

vegetable oil
Caramel Coating (see page 133)
275 g (10 oz) hazelnuts, pecans,
walnuts or unsalted peanuts or a
combination
350 g (12 oz) plain chocolate, chopped
2 tbsp white vegetable fat

◆ Oil 2 baking sheets with the vegetable oil. Prepare the caramel coating.

◆ When the caramel has cooled for a few minutes, stir in the nuts until they are coated. Do not overwork or the caramel will crystallize. Using an oiled tablespoon, drop spoonfuls of caramel-nut mixture on to the prepared baking sheet, about 2.5 cm (1 inch) apart. If the caramel-nut mixture becomes too hard, reheat over low heat for several minutes until softened. Refrigerate until firm and cold.

◆ Using a palette knife, transfer the nut clusters to a wire rack over a baking sheet to catch the drips. In a saucepan over a low heat, melt the chocolate and vegetable fat, stirring occasionally until smooth; cool the chocolate to about 30°C (88°F).

◆ Using a tablespoon, spoon the chocolate over the nut clusters, being sure to coat completely, spreading the chocolate over the surface. Return the drips to the saucepan and reheat gently to completely cover all the clusters. Leave to set for about 2 hours at room temperature. Store in a cool place in an airtight container with foil between the layers, but do not refrigerate.

Chocolate-Dipped Fruit

MAKES ABOUT 12

*about 12 pieces of fruit, such as
strawberries; cherries; orange
segments; kiwi fruit; fresh peeled
lychees; Cape gooseberries; stoned
prunes; stoned dates; dried apricots;
dried pears; nuts*
*175 g (6 oz) good-quality white
chocolate, chopped*
75 g (3 oz) plain chocolate, chopped

◆ Clean and prepare the fruit. Wipe
the strawberries with a soft cloth or
brush gently with a pastry brush;
wash and dry firm-skinned fruits such
as cherries and grapes. Dry well and
set on paper towels to absorb any
remaining moisture. Peel or cut any
other fruits being used. Dried or
candied fruits can also be used.
◆ In the top of a double boiler over a
low heat, melt the white chocolate,
stirring frequently until smooth.
Remove from heat and cool to tepid,
about 28°C (84°F), stirring frequently.
◆ Line a baking sheet with
greaseproof paper or foil. Holding the
fruit by the stem or end and at an
angle, dip about two-thirds of the fruit
into the chocolate. Allow the excess to
drip off and place on the baking
sheet. Continue dipping the fruit; if
the chocolate becomes too thick, set
over hot water again briefly to soften
slightly. Refrigerate the fruit until the
chocolate sets, about 20 minutes.

◆ In the top of the cleaned double
boiler over low heat, melt the plain
chocolate, stirring frequently until
smooth. Remove from the heat and
cool to just below body temperature,
about 30°C (88°F).
◆ Remove each white chocolate-
coated fruit from the baking sheet
and holding each by the stem or end,
and at the opposite angle, dip the
bottom third of each piece into the
dark chocolate, creating a chevron
effect. Set on the baking sheet.
Refrigerate for 5 minutes, or until set.
Remove from the refrigerator 10-15
minutes before serving to soften the
chocolate.

Chocolate-Coated Toffee

MAKES ABOUT 750 G (1½ LB)

150 g (5 oz) pecans (optional)
225 g (8 oz) unsalted butter,
cut into pieces
350 g (12 oz) sugar
1.5 ml (¼ tsp) cream of tartar
175 g (6 oz) plain chocolate,
finely chopped

◆ Preheat the oven to 180°C (350°F, Gas Mark 4). Place the pecans (if using) on a small baking sheet and bake for 10-12 minutes, until well toasted. Leave to cool completely, then chop and set aside.

◆ Line a 23 cm (9 inch) square cake tin with foil. Invert the tin and mould the foil over the bottom. Turn the tin right side up and line with the moulded foil. Generously butter the bottom and sides of the foil.
◆ In a heavy-based saucepan over a medium heat, melt the butter. Stir in the sugar and cream of tartar, stirring until the sugar dissolves. Bring the mixture to the boil. Cover the pan for 2 minutes so steam washes down any sugar crystals which collect on the side of the pan. Uncover and continue cooking for 10-12 minutes, or until the toffee reaches 154°C (310°F) on a sweet thermometer.

◆ Carefully pour into the tin and leave to rest for about 1 minute. Sprinkle the top of the toffee with chocolate and leave for 2 minutes until the chocolate softens. Using the back of a spoon or a wide-bladed knife, spread the chocolate evenly over the toffee until smooth. Sprinkle evenly with the chopped pecans (if using). Cool to room temperature, then refrigerate until firm and cold.
◆ Using the foil as a guide, remove the toffee from the tin. With the back of a heavy knife or hammer, break the toffee into large, irregular pieces.

RIGHT *Chocolate-Coated Toffee*

Chocolate Eggs

MAKES 4

4 medium eggs
225 g (8 oz) plain or milk chocolate
75 g (3 oz) praline, ground finely
30 ml (2 tbsp) cream

◆ Using an egg prick or pin, pierce a hole at the pointed end of each egg.
◆ Using small scissors, carefully enlarge the hole to about 1 cm (½ inch).
◆ Push a cocktail stick or toothpick into the hole to puncture the yolk. Shake the raw egg into a bowl.
◆ Run water gently into the shells and shake until they are clean. Turn upside down and leave to dry.
◆ Melt the chocolate. Stir in the praline and cream. Spoon or pour the chocolate into the dry shells. Leave until set.
◆ Seal the holes with small round labels and place the eggs in an egg box, holed side down.

Chocolate-Mint Crisps

MAKES ABOUT 30

vegetable oil for greasing
4 tbsp sugar
60 ml (2 fl oz) water
5 ml (1 tsp) peppermint essence
225 g (8 oz) plain chocolate, chopped

◆ Grease a baking sheet with vegetable oil. Set aside. In a saucepan, bring the sugar and water to the boil, swirling the pan until the sugar dissolves. Boil rapidly until the sugar reaches 140°C (280°F) on a sugar thermometer. Remove the pan from the heat and stir in the peppermint essence. Pour on to the greased baking sheet and allow to set; do not touch as the sugar syrup is very hot and can cause serious burns.

◆ When the mixture is cold, use a rolling pin to break it up into pieces. Place the pieces into a food processor fitted with the metal blade and process until fine crumbs form; do not overprocess.

◆ Line 2 baking sheets with greaseproof paper or foil; grease the paper or foil. In the top of a double boiler over a low heat, melt the chocolate, stirring frequently until smooth. Remove from the heat and stir in the ground mint mixture.

◆ Using a teaspoon, drop small mounds of mixture on to the prepared baking sheets. Using the back of the spoon, spread into 2.5 cm (1 inch) circles. Cool, then refrigerate to set, at least 1 hour. Peel off the paper or foil and store in airtight containers with greaseproof paper between each layer. Store in the refrigerator for 1 week.

Chocolate-Stuffed Figs and Prunes

MAKES 24

12 large fresh figs
12 extra-large stoned prunes,
preferably presoaked or softened
40 g (1½ oz) unsalted butter, softened
75 g (3 oz) blanched almonds,
chopped and toasted
1 egg yolk
15 ml (1 tbsp) Amaretto liqueur
75 g (3 oz) plain chocolate, melted and
cooled

Chocolate for dipping
225 g (8 oz) plain chocolate, chopped
65 g (2½ oz) unsalted butter,
cut into pieces

◆ In a food processor fitted with the metal blade, process the butter, almonds, egg yolk and liqueur until creamy. With the machine running, slowly pour in the melted chocolate and process until well blended. Scrape into a bowl and refrigerate for about 1 hour, until firm enough to pipe.

◆ Line a baking sheet with greaseproof paper. Pipe the mixture into the figs and prunes. Place the filled fruits on the baking sheet and chill for 30 minutes.

◆ In a saucepan over a low heat, melt the chocolate and butter, stirring frequently until melted and smooth. Leave to cool to room temperature, about 30 minutes, stirring occasionally.

◆ Insert a cocktail stick into each filled fruit. Dip each into the melted chocolate and allow the excess to drip off. Using another cocktail stick, push the fruit off the inserted cocktail stick on to the lined baking sheet. Alternatively, dip the filled fruits about two-thirds of the way into the chocolate, leaving one-third exposed. Place on the baking sheet. Refrigerate for at least 1 hour to set.

◆ Using a thin-bladed knife, remove the fruit from the baking sheet to paper cases. Remove from the refrigerator about 30 minutes before serving.

White Chocolate Fudge Layer

MAKES 36 TRIANGLES

600 g (1¼ lb) good-quality white
chocolate, chopped
400 g (14 oz) can sweetened condensed
milk
10 ml (2 tsp) vanilla essence
7.5 ml (1½ tsp) white vinegar or lemon
juice
pinch of salt
250 g (9 oz) unsalted macadamia nuts
175 g (6 oz) plain chocolate, chopped
40 g (1½ oz) unsalted butter,
cut into pieces
25 g (1 oz) plain chocolate, melted,
for piping

◆ Line a 20 cm (8 inch) square cake
tin with foil. Invert the tin. Mould the
foil over the bottom, then turn the
cake tin right side up and line with
the foil. Grease the bottom and sides
of the foil. Set aside.
◆ In a saucepan over a low heat,
melt the chocolate with the
condensed milk, stirring frequently
until smooth. Remove from the heat
and stir in the vanilla essence,
vinegar and salt until well blended.
Stir in the nuts. Spread half of the
white chocolate mixture in the tin.
Refrigerate for 15 minutes or until
firm; keep the remaining mixture
warm.
◆ In a saucepan over a low heat,
melt the chopped chocolate and
butter, stirring frequently until
smooth. Cool slightly; pour over the
white chocolate layer and refrigerate
until firm, about 15 minutes.

◆ If necessary, gently reheat the
remaining white chocolate mixture
then pour over the set chocolate
layer, smoothing the top evenly.
Refrigerate for 2-4 hours, until
completely firm.
◆ Using the foil as a guide, remove
the set fudge from the tin. With a
knife, cut into 16 squares. Cut each
square diagonally in half, making 36
triangles. Place the fudge triangles on
to a wire rack placed over a baking
sheet to catch the drips.
◆ Spoon the melted chocolate into a
small paper cone and drizzle
chocolate over the fudge triangles.
Store in an airtight container in the
refrigerator for 1-2 weeks.

RIGHT *White Chocolate Fudge Layer*

Rocky Road Fudge

MAKES ABOUT 750 G (1½ LB)

450 g (1 lb) milk chocolate
50 g (2 oz) butter
30 ml (2 tbsp) single cream
5 ml (1 tsp) vanilla essence
50 g (2 oz) walnuts, chopped
100 g (4 oz) marshmallows, cut into
small pieces with wetted scissors
225 g (8 oz) icing sugar, sieved
75 g (3 oz) plain chocolate, to decorate

◆ Melt the chocolate and butter in a
bowl over a pan of hot water. Stir in
the cream and vanilla essence.
◆ Remove from the heat and stir in
the walnuts, marshmallows and icing
sugar.
◆ Spread in a 20 cm (8 inch) square
tin, lined with greaseproof paper.
◆ Chill until firm.
◆ Melt the plain chocolate. Using a
piping bag fitted with a plain nozzle,
drizzle the chocolate over the fudge.
Leave to set.
◆ To serve, cut the fudge into
diamond shapes.

Easy Chocolate Truffles

MAKES ABOUT 45

150 ml (5 fl oz) whipping cream
250 g (9 oz) plain chocolate, chopped
30 ml (2 tbsp) brandy or other liqueur
(optional)
50 g (2 oz) cocoa powder

◆ In a saucepan over a low heat, bring the cream to the boil. Remove the pan from the heat. Add the chocolate all at once, stirring frequently until smooth. Stir in the liqueur if using. Strain into a bowl and cool to room temperature. Refrigerate for 1 hour, until thickened and firm.

◆ Line 2 small baking sheets with foil. Using a melon baller, a 2.5 cm (1 inch) ice-cream scoop or a teaspoon, form the mixture into 2.5 cm (1 inch) balls and place on the baking sheets. Refrigerate for 1-2 hours, until the balls are firm.

◆ Place the cocoa powder in a small bowl. Drop each chocolate ball into the cocoa and turn with your fingers to coat with cocoa. Roll the balls between the palms of your hands, dusting with more cocoa if necessary. Do not try to make them perfectly round; they should look slightly irregular. Place on the baking sheets. Add more cocoa to the bowl if necessary.

◆ Shake the cocoa-coated truffles in a dry sieve to remove excess cocoa, then store, covered, in the refrigerator for up to 2 weeks or freeze for up to 2 months. Soften for 10 minutes at room temperature before serving.

Chocolate-Coated Raspberry Truffles

MAKES ABOUT 24

625 g (22 oz) bittersweet chocolate,
chopped
75 g (3 oz) unsalted butter,
cut into pieces
75 ml (2½ fl oz) seedless raspberry jam
30 ml (2 tbsp) raspberry-flavour
liqueur
350 g (12 oz) chocolate, chopped

◆ In a saucepan over low heat, melt 275 g (10 oz) chocolate, butter and jam, stirring frequently until smooth and well blended. Remove from the heat and stir in the liqueur. Strain into a bowl and cool. Refrigerate for 2-3 hours, until firm.

◆ Line a baking sheet with greaseproof paper or foil. Using a melon baller, a 2.5 cm (1 inch) ice-cream scoop or a teaspoon, form the mixture into balls. Place on the baking sheet and freeze for 1 hour, or until very firm.

◆ In the top of a double boiler over low heat, melt the remaining chocolate, stirring frequently until smooth; the chocolate should be 46-48°C (115°-120°F). Remove from the heat and pour into a clean bowl; cool to about 30°C (88°F).

◆ Using a fork, dip the truffles, 1 at a time, into the chocolate, coating completely and tapping the fork on the edge of the bowl to shake off the excess. Place on the prepared baking sheet. Refrigerate until the chocolate is set, about 1 hour. Store in an airtight container with paper towels covering the truffles to collect any moisture for up to 2 weeks or 1 month in freezer.

Milk Chocolate and Pistachio-Coated Truffles

MAKES ABOUT 24

120 ml (4 fl oz) double or whipping cream
350 g (12 oz) good-quality milk chocolate, chopped
15 g (½ oz) unsalted butter
15 ml (1 tbsp) almond- or hazelnut-flavour liqueur
350 g (12 oz) bittersweet chocolate, chopped
150 g (5 oz) shelled and unsalted pistachio nuts, finely chopped

◆ In a medium saucepan over a medium heat, bring the cream to the boil. Remove from the heat. Add the chocolate all at once, stirring until melted. Stir in the butter and liqueur. Strain into a bowl. Refrigerate for 1 hour or until firm.

◆ Line a baking sheet with greaseproof paper or foil. Using a melon baller, a 2.5 cm (1 inch) ice-cream scoop or a teaspoon, form the mixture into balls. Place on a baking sheet and freeze for 1 hour, or until very firm.

◆ In the top of a double boiler over a low heat, melt the bittersweet chocolate, stirring frequently until smooth; the chocolate should be about 46-48°C (115°-120°F). Remove from the heat and pour into a clean bowl; cool to about 30°C (88°F).

◆ Place the pistachios in a bowl. Using a fork, dip the truffles, 1 at a time, into the chocolate, coating completely and tapping the fork on the edge of the bowl to shake off the excess. Immediately drop into the bowl of pistachios and roll to coat the chocolate completely. Place on the prepared baking sheet. Refrigerate until set, about 1 hour. Store in an airtight container with paper towels covering the truffles to collect any moisture for up to 2 weeks or 1 month in the freezer.

RIGHT *Milk Chocolate and Pistachio-Coated Truffles*

Rich Chocolate Truffles

MAKES ABOUT 30

225 g (8 oz) plain or milk chocolate
100 g (4 oz) butter, diced
10 ml (2 tsp) liqueur (eg Tia Maria, Cointreau, rum or brandy)
175 g (6 oz) icing sugar
ground nuts

◆ Melt the chocolate. Remove from the heat.

◆ Add the butter and liqueur and beat until smooth.

◆ Beat in the icing sugar.

◆ Chill well until firm.

◆ Shape into 2.5 cm (1 inch) balls and roll in the nuts.

◆ To serve, place in paper cases and keep cool.

AUCES

Tobler Sauce   149

Chocolate Sauce   150

Chocolate Syrup   150

Fudge Sauce   151

Chocolate Custard   151

Mars Bar Sauce   151

Tobler Sauce

SERVES 4

225 g (8 oz) Toblerone chocolate
150 ml (¼ pt) double cream

◆ Cut the chocolate into very small pieces. Put into a small pan and melt very quickly.
◆ Stir in the cream. Mix until smooth and immediately pour over ice cream or fruit such as bananas or pears.

SWEET SUCCESS

If you need to use the same baking sheets to bake in batches, cool by running the back of the baking sheet under cold water and wiping the surface with a paper towel before regreasing.

Chocolate Sauce

SERVES 3-4

50 g (2 oz) cocoa powder
4 tbsp golden syrup
50 g (2 oz) butter
150 ml (¼ pt) milk
2.5 ml (½ tsp) vanilla essence

◆ Put the cocoa, golden syrup and butter into a small pan. Heat gently until well blended.
◆ Stir in the milk and vanilla essence.
◆ Bring to the boil and simmer gently for about 3 minutes. Serve hot or cold.

> VARIATIONS
>
> **Chocolate/Orange Sauce:** Omit the vanilla essence. Add the grated zest of ½ orange.

Chocolate Syrup

SERVES 3-4

350 g (12 oz) soft brown sugar
100 g (4 oz) cocoa powder
300 ml (½ pt) boiling water
10 ml (2 tsp) vanilla essence

◆ Mix together the sugar and cocoa.
◆ Add the water, stirring continuously.
◆ Put the mixture into a small pan and simmer gently for 5 minutes, stirring frequently.
◆ Cool. Add the vanilla essence.
◆ Cover and chill in the refrigerator.

FUDGE SAUCE

CHOCOLATE SAUCE

CHOCOLATE SYRUP

Fudge Sauce

SERVES 4-6

15 ml (1 tbsp) cocoa powder
175 g (6 oz) can evaporated milk
75 g (3 oz) plain chocolate, grated
25 g (1 oz) butter
25 g (1 oz) soft brown sugar

◆ Put the cocoa and evaporated milk into a pan and whisk well together.
◆ Add all the remaining ingredients. Heat gently, stirring, until the chocolate, sugar and butter have melted. Do not boil. Serve hot or warm.

Chocolate Custard

MAKES 600 ML (1 PT)

600 ml (1 pt) milk
6 egg yolks
50 g (2 oz) sugar
100 g (4 oz) plain chocolate, grated

◆ Put the milk into a saucepan and bring almost to the boil. Remove from the heat.
◆ Whisk the egg yolks and sugar together until thick and fluffy.
◆ Gradually pour the milk on to the eggs and sugar, whisking continuously.
◆ Return the mixture to the saucepan and stir over a very gentle heat, until it coats the back of a spoon.

◆ Remove from the heat and add the chocolate. Stir until dissolved.
◆ Serve the custard hot or cold. To cool the custard, pour into a bowl and place dampened greaseproof paper directly on to the surface to stop a skin from forming. Chill.

Mars Bar Sauce

SERVES 4

4 Mars Bars
90 ml (6 tbsp) double cream

◆ Dice the Mars Bars. Put in a small pan and melt very gently.
◆ Stir in the cream. Mix until smooth and immediately pour over ice cream.

RINKS

Deluxe Chocolate Egg Nog

SERVES 10-12

250 g (9 oz) plain chocolate, chopped
475 ml (16 fl oz) milk
6 eggs
50 g (2 oz) sugar
120 ml (4 fl oz) brandy or rum
120 ml (4 fl oz) Amaretto liqueur
30 ml (2 tbsp) vanilla essence
475 ml (16 fl oz) whipping cream
grated chocolate or cocoa powder
to decorate

◆ In a saucepan over a low heat, melt the chocolate and 250 ml (8 fl oz) milk, stirring frequently until smooth. Remove from the heat and stir in the remaining cold milk until well blended. Cool to room temperature.

◆ With an electric mixer, beat the eggs and sugar until pale and thick, 5-7 minutes. Gradually beat in the cooled chocolate, brandy, liqueur and vanilla essence.

◆ In another bowl, with a hand-held electric mixer, beat the whipping cream just until soft peaks form. Stir a spoonful of cream into the chocolate-egg mixture then fold in the remaining cream. Chill.

VARIATION

To prepare without alcohol, omit the brandy and liqueur and substitute 250 ml (8 fl oz) milk, chocolate milk or cream.

Continental Hot Chocolate

MAKES 1 CUP

40 g (1½ oz) plain chocolate, chopped
1½ tsp cocoa powder
pinch of salt
½ tsp sugar
milk

◆ Place the chocolate, cocoa powder, salt and sugar in a small saucepan. Take the cup in which the chocolate will be served, fill it about one-quarter full of milk and then add enough water to almost fill the cup.

◆ Add the milk and water to the saucepan and, over medium heat, bring to a boil, beating constantly until the chocolate is melted and smooth. Boil for 30 seconds longer, beating until foamy, then pour into the cup. Serve immediately.

Spicy Hot Cocoa

SERVES 4

75 g (3 oz) sugar
40 g (1½ oz) cocoa powder
½ tsp grated nutmeg
½ tsp ground cloves
½ tsp ground ginger
120 ml (4 fl oz) cold water
7.5 cm (3 inch) cinnamon stick,
broken into pieces
5 ml (1 tsp) vanilla essence
900 ml (1½ pt) milk
marshmallows or whipped cream to
decorate

◆ In a saucepan, combine the sugar, cocoa powder, nutmeg, cloves and ginger. Gradually stir in the water until the mixture is smooth. Add the cinnamon pieces and bring to the boil, stirring constantly. Cook for 1 minute longer, stirring constantly.

◆ Gradually beat in the milk and bring the mixture to below the boil (do not boil), beating constantly until the mixture is frothy. Remove from the heat, beat in the vanilla essence and strain into large cups or mugs. Top each with a few marshmallows or a dollop of whipped cream.

VARIATION

Minty Hot Chocolate: Prepare as above but omit the nutmeg, cloves, ginger, cinnamon and vanilla. After the milk is beaten in, beat in 30 ml (2 tbsp) mint-flavour liqueur or 15 ml (1 tbsp) peppermint essence.

Velvety Hot Chocolate

SERVES 2

100 g (4 oz) plain chocolate, chopped
45 ml (3 tbsp) cold water
30 ml (2 tbsp) hot water
475 ml (16 fl oz) milk
whipped cream to decorate

◆ In the top of a double boiler over a low heat, melt the chocolate and cold water, stirring frequently until smooth. Remove from the heat and beat in the hot water, beating until smooth. Pour into a small pitcher or 2 large cups or mugs.

◆ In a saucepan, bring the milk to the boil and pour into a separate pitcher, or pour some of the milk into each cup or mug of chocolate. Top with whipped cream. Serve at once.

Rich Iced Chocolate

SERVES 2

250 ml (8 fl oz) whipping cream
100 g (4 oz) plain chocolate, chopped
10 ml (2 tsp) vanilla essence
475 ml (16 fl oz) freshly brewed
espresso coffee, chilled
sugar to taste
grated chocolate to decorate (optional)

◆ In a small saucepan over a medium heat, bring the cream to the boil. Add the chocolate all at once, stirring until smooth. Remove from the heat and stir in the vanilla essence. Strain into a bowl. Cool to room temperature. Refrigerate for about 1 hour to chill but do not allow the chocolate to set.

◆ To serve, beat the cold espresso coffee into the chilled chocolate until well blended and frothy. Fill 2 tall glasses one-quarter full with crushed ice, then pour the chocolate-coffee mixture over. Sprinkle with grated chocolate.

Extra-Chocolate Milk Shake

SERVES 2

50 g (2 oz) cocoa powder
100 g (4 oz) sugar
120 ml (4 fl oz) water
75 ml (2½ fl oz) golden syrup
5 ml (1 tsp) vanilla essence
120 ml (4 fl oz) cold milk
15 ml (1 tbsp) chocolate-flavour
liqueur
300 ml (10 fl oz) chocolate ice cream
chocolate curls or grated chocolate
to decorate

◆ First make the chocolate syrup. In a saucepan over a medium heat, combine the cocoa and sugar. Gradually stir in the water until smooth and well blended. Stir in the golden syrup, then bring to the boil, stirring frequently.

◆ Cook for 2-3 minutes, stirring constantly, until the mixture is smooth and thickened. Remove from the heat and stir in the vanilla essence. Cool slightly.

◆ In a blender or milk-shake machine, combine the milk, chocolate syrup and liqueur (if using). Blend for 30 seconds. Add the ice cream and blend for about 45 seconds, just until smooth. Pour into 2 tall glasses and decorate with chocolate curls or grated chocolate.

Chocolate Cream Liqueur

MAKES ABOUT 1.1 LITRES (2 PT)

1 tbsp instant coffee powder
25 g (1 oz) cocoa powder
250 ml (8 fl oz) milk
250 ml (8 fl oz) double cream
400 g (14 oz) can condensed milk
1 egg yolk
250 ml (8 fl oz) whisky
75 ml (2½ fl oz) light rum
15 ml (1 tbsp) vanilla essence
15 ml (1 tbsp) coconut essence

◆ In a large, heavy-based saucepan, combine the coffee and cocoa powders. Gradually stir in the milk until the powders are dissolved. Stir in the cream and condensed milk and bring to the boil.

◆ In a bowl, lightly beat the egg yolk. Pour about 250 ml (8 fl oz) hot cream mixture over the egg yolk, beating well, then stir the cream-and-egg mixture back into the pan. Cook for 2-3 minutes longer until the mixture thickens and coats the back of a spoon. Remove from the heat. Stir in the whisky, rum and vanilla and coconut essences. Strain into a bowl and cool to room temperature, stirring occasionally. Refrigerate for 2-3 hours until well chilled.

◆ Transfer to a bottle or jar with a tight-fitting lid and store in the refrigerator. Shake before serving.

FROM TOP RIGHT, CLOCKWISE: *Continental Hot Chocolate, Spicy Hot Cocoa* and *Velvety Hot Chocolate*

Iced Caribbean Chocolate

SERVES 4

400 ml (¾ pt) milk
150 ml (¼ pt) single cream
2 large pinches of ground nutmeg
2 large pinches of ground cinnamon
1 large pinch of ground allspice
5 tbsp Chocolate Syrup (see page 150)

To serve
ice cubes
coffee ice cream

◆ Put the milk, cream, spices and syrup into a bowl and whisk well together. Chill well.
◆ Before serving, whisk again.
◆ To serve, pour into glasses over ice cubes and top with scoops of coffee ice cream.

Choconana Milk Shake

SERVES 2-3

300 ml (½ pt) milk
3 tbsp Chocolate Syrup (see page 150)
600 ml (1 pt) chocolate ice cream
1 banana, cut into pieces
bought chocolate flake bars to serve

◆ Put the milk, chocolate syrup, ice cream and banana into a blender.
◆ Cover and blend until smooth.
◆ To serve, pour into glasses and add a chocolate flake to each one.

ICED CARIBBEAN CHOCOLATE

CHOCONANA MILK SHAKE

$\mathcal{I}$NDEX